"I will not be erased"

WITH ILLUSTRATIONS BY JESS NASH

First published 2019 by Walker Books Ltd
87 Vauxhall Walk, London SE11 5HJ

10 9 8 7 6 5 4 3 2

Anthology © 2019 gal-dem

gal-dem have asserted their moral rights

This book has been typeset in Futura

Printed and bound by CPI Group (UK) Ltd,
Croydon CR0 4YY

British Library Cataloguing in Publication Data:
a catalogue record for this book is available from
the British Library

ISBN 978-1-4063-8637-0

www.walker.co.uk

www.gal-dem.com

"I will not be erased"

Our stories about growing up as people of colour

gal-dem

WALKER
BOOKS

contents

a letter from gal-dem's editors

We're gal-dem, a magazine written and produced exclusively by young women and non-binary people of colour. This is the first time we've published a book, and it is the book we wish had existed when we were growing up.

So many of us felt the sting of erasure when we were young. We didn't see ourselves in literature or comics, in TV or film, or in the world around us. Our voices and experiences were missing from the history books and from positions of power. We know that many of our younger siblings and friends are still struggling with validation because of this erasure. And even though we've (almost) grown up sometimes we struggle too. The title of our book is a powerful statement to you and to ourselves: we refuse to be erased, and we are working hard so that you don't have to feel that you have been either. With this book we want to show you that your voice matters and your experiences are important.

There is something in each of these essays that will speak to anyone who has ever wondered what they might say to their younger self. After all, we've all fallen in love, fought with our parents or wondered where we fit in. But it is our hope that these essays will especially speak to those of us from marginalized backgrounds. Growing up as black, brown, East Asian, Arab or as any other minority identity in a majority white society, we feel we have had to contend with some unique experiences. But we have rarely seen those experiences written about in something as tangible as a book, and we want to change that.

Each essay in this collection is inspired by something we wrote when we were growing up. We've taken our diary entries and screenshotted conversations, poems and messages from faded notepads or school diary planners that we've never quite been able to throw away. We've all written about an experience that shaped us in some way and made us who we are today. We hope you can learn from our adventures, mistakes and heartbreaks so you feel less alone in your struggles and more at home in your joy.

We've all been on very different journeys. A diary is where you get to define yourself on your own terms and take control of your narrative. What you write leaves a legacy. We hope our pasts and our futures speak as one about secret angst, anger and embarrassment, but also of life's ridiculous joy and humour. Some of us have realized that we aren't so different from our younger selves; others have life lessons we want to share because of how much we have changed.

Sometimes it feels like there's no one in your world who you can speak to: no one who really understands or who wants to listen. One of the things we've discovered about growing up is that there is almost always someone out there. And if not? Writing down your feelings and experiences is a good place to start.

by Charlie Brinkhurst-Cuff

and Liv Little

RACISM AND REVENGE

ALWAYS BE BIGGER THAN YOUR BULLIES

written by

YUMNA
AL-ARASHI

12 July 2003

This morning my dad woke me up earlier than I needed and he was really pissed off. He told me to come downstairs and I went down and followed him outside. There was toilet paper all over our tree and styrofoam plates of actual shit on our driveway. He showed me someone left a note on our door that said "I thought this is what your people eat for breakfast."

I hate being here. I hate McLean. I hate everyone here. My only friends that get me are Christine and Izzy and they hate it here too. I can't wait till I'm a senior and can go to NYC.

I don't know what to do. I hate this. My dad is so fed up. Last week someone left a dead possum on our doorstep. And this is the second time someone toilet-papered our house. He thinks it's my fault and that I'm bringing trouble to me.

I think it's JS and L. I'm going to kill them. They're such LOSERS. If they have problems with ME then why are they doing this to my DAD'S HOUSE. They should talk to my face and not act like such losers.

Diary entry: age 14

Sweet Yumna,

The slam of your bedroom door was so loud that I thought I'd come check in on you. It's me, you, sixteen years from now. I see that you've locked yourself in your bedroom after a pretty rough day. Well, maybe a pretty rough few years. I see you screaming into your pillow and wondering why you even exist. I see you. You're fourteen and you are angry. I'm thirty now and I'm writing to you because, in this moment, you think you are completely alone in this strange world. I know you can't imagine having to deal with it for any longer, but look, you've made it this far. And you'll make it further yet.

Two years ago, the whole world flipped upside down. On September 11 2001, America was struck by a series of horrible events which shook the country. Hijacked planes crashed into the World Trade Center in New York, the Pentagon in Washington DC and a field in Pennsylvania, and many people were killed. Tensions began to rise between the Western world and the Middle East. Up until that point, Yumna, you were just another kid in the suburbs of Washington DC: you went to school, you played instruments, you had friends, you played soccer. After that horrific morning, you were from the same place as the terrorists, your father worked for an Arab government, your skin was brown, you were Muslim and your holiday trips to see family in the Middle East were suddenly questioned. For the first time in your life, you were different.

It was weird to realize that you were from the same place as people who'd done something so damaging to the country you were born in. It was heartbreaking to learn that people could have such bad intentions. But, through all of this confusion and hurt, you've started to learn some harsh lessons about the politics of the world. Sometimes those in power choose to target a specific group of people as a way to justify their actions, and to make a show of revenge. There's a darker side to the power structures of this world and, although it feels horrible, this will inspire you to fight for fair treatment of all.

You, Yumna, are a clever little creature and you have a desperate need to learn. Pain and trauma will be the keys that open a door to learning about your place in the world. Your job will be to help defend all those who have been shamed because of the actions of a few. Although it doesn't seem like it right now, this is the greatest gift to you because it will inspire you to work harder, and feel deeper.

The next few years as a young teen will not be easy. Going to school has never been your favourite way to spend your time, and your schoolmates are now far and few between. Kids can be evil, and I'm sorry to say that you will come into contact with some of the worst kind: bullies.

One month from today, the summer holidays will be over and you'll be back in school for another year of dread. A few days later, a boy, let's call him Jamie Smith, will throw a full, open bottle of water at the back of your head. You will feel your first taste of absolute rage and it will finally click that it was him harassing you, your family and your home over the last year.

No, it is not cool that he has toilet-papered your house twice now. It is definitely not cool that he burned a live animal on your doorstep. And it is straight-up disgusting that he has spent the time leaving faeces in your driveway. Let me say this loud and clear: THERE IS NOTHING OK ABOUT JAMIE SMITH. He is an outright horrible person and the people around him applauding his actions are weak humans he's manipulated into being his friends. This goes further than bullying. This is hate crime. You in no way, shape or form deserve the treatment he's given you.

The day he throws the water bottle at your head, you will snap.

After school, while he's on "The White Path", where the cool kids go to hang out

"You in no way, shape or form deserve the treatment he's given you."

behind the school, smoking cigarettes with the rest of the losers who will end up doing nothing with their lives, you will lash out and beat him up in front of all of his friends. He will punch you back in the face.

Now, I understand your anger. But this is not the appropriate way to handle the situation. You should take a few breaths and try to ease that anger before making heated decisions. I know that you will feel there is nothing else you can do to make this stupid boy stop harassing you. I know you will think your only option is to take physical action, but let me remind you that you are living in a place where your every action is judged. If you physically attack someone, no matter how deserving you believe your action is, you will only continue a vicious cycle of racism. Others are waiting to call you an angry terrorist; they think that people like you are always violent. Prove them wrong with your patience.

But the heat of the moment will force you into a corner and your emotions will run over. You will do it anyway.

The next morning, you will be called into the principal's office to explain your side of what happened. Your friends who witnessed the fight will also testify to the pain Jamie has caused you which has led you to take this action. You will be suspended from school. He will not. You will experience your first interaction with institutionalized racism.

You will wonder: did they not see your scabbed nose from the punch he threw? Were you too upset to explain fully that the bottle he'd thrown at your head was full of water? Did you mention that he burned a live animal on your doorstep? How is it that you are suspended and he is not?

"You will be suspended from school. He will not. You will experience your first interaction with institutionalized racism."

Sweet Yumna, the anger you feel today will multiply by the hundreds. You will question yourself. You will question a system that is supposed to have your back. You will question whether or not your friends did defend you when they were speaking to the principal. You will wonder what Jamie Smith will do next.

I want you to know that it is OK to be this angry, but please remember that you do nothing to deserve this. Your friends love you and will be by your side for the rest of your life. They are your family: keep them close. It's a question of what you will do now with your anger.

The majority of people at your school are white, including the administration. People throw the word "terrorist" at you like it's a joke. Because you physically attack Jamie Smith, the administration of your school will feel the only right thing to do is reprimand you, the Arab, for being "violent". They will advise your father that you will "be watched".

I know you might not realize it just yet, but this is racism. Please, calmly call everyone out when they use the word "terrorist" to describe you. It is a racially derogatory word. They have no idea the weight it carries inside of you and will never understand because they are blinded by their own privileges.

Don't let this break you. Your dad is on your side, and although he's angry right now, it is because he loves you and hates to see you being bullied. Explain, in great detail, what Jamie Smith has done to you. He might have a solution a lot more powerful than your emotional rage.

The only adult on your side at school during this traumatic experience will be Mr Stokely, an African American police officer. You will realize that Mr Stokely has an attentiveness to detail when he asks you questions that the rest of the administration does not. Mr Stokely will personally go to your house and apologize to your father for what has happened as a result of Jamie Smith's actions. He will inform your father that Jamie has not only targeted you but many others in the school. He will let your father know that it is Jamie who is being watched, not you. In a few years, this man, your saviour Mr Stokely, will be the one to put Jamie Smith in jail after he is involved in a drink-driving accident and seriously hurts a young family in the other car.

You will learn what solidarity means.

Over the next and last few years of school in DC, your anger will harden your heart towards your town and your school. You will want to escape and will try to find various ways of doing so. You might skip class so much that you almost do not graduate. I get it, Yumna. It's not easy. Find solace away from school learning about the complexities of the world around you and why these complexities exist. Speak to your father more – he may be suffering from the same pains you are but in his work environment. You can be there for one another, and it will be beautiful. His age and social status mean he will be taken far more seriously than you. He can help you, and he will.

The day after you graduate high school, you will move to New York. It will seem like a dream, and you'll be surrounded by beautiful, inspiring people. This is the place where all those like you have come to find one another, and you'll feel a peace that you've never felt before. For the first time, you won't feel alone.

Racism and ignorance will continue to grow in America and, trust me, sometimes it will

"This is the place where all those like you have come to find one another."

feel like it is only getting worse. Speaking live from the future, I can tell you that things look pretty bleak. But for the amount of stupidity this world can offer, you will find an equal amount of solidarity along the way – always. Feed your brain, learn your histories, and take care of yourself. Escapes, like drugs and alcohol, are temporary, and you will always have to pay for them by facing an even darker void soon after you try to run away. Don't go there.

Instead, you will learn how to control your temper and fight back with your wisdom and art. But please, don't forget to love yourself along the way. You are so smart, so powerful, and you have so much to offer this world. Don't let insecurities hold you back.

Over the years, you will realize that the media has shaped so much of others' perceptions of who you are. Your job is to unlearn the noise and the messages you have internalized, and ask people to join you along your journey. You will inspire so many more like you to fight back with wit and courage, not violence. Your gold will be the generous and inspirational people you meet along the way, the knowledge you gain, and your family. Stay opinionated and do not ever hide the strength that has been inside you since birth. Always question the world around you and never accept the easiest way out. This includes acting on pure emotion. That's too easy, and you're smarter than that.

It's OK to make mistakes. But learn from them.
Try to be a better version of yourself every day.
You're going to be so, so brilliant.

Love,

Yumna

"For the amount of stupidity
this world can offer,
you will find an equal
amount of solidarity
along the way — always."

some names have been changed

"IT'S POM-MANG-GRANATE"

BE PROUD OF WHAT MAKES YOUR STORY DIFFERENT

written by

SAMANTHI THEMINIMULLE

Today at school everyone laughed
at me because I said pomangranate.
Apparently it's pomegranate.
Ammi and Appachchi say pomangranate????
So embarrassing.
I've always said it wrong.

Diary entry: age 14

Hi, fourteen-year-old me,

It's tough being the child of immigrant parents –
there's nothing worse than being made to feel like
you're different from everyone else. Do you remember
when you pronounced "pomegranate" wrong in front
of the entire class and everyone laughed? How did
that go again?

Class:	*What did you just say?*
Me:	*I said my mum packed me some pom-mang-granate for lunch.*
Class:	*Um. Sam. What is a pom-mang-granate?*
Me:	*You've never heard of a pom-mang-granate? The small red seeds? Here, look, like this.*
Class:	*OMG ARE YOU DUMB? THAT'S CALLED "POMEGRANATE". POM-MANG-GRANATE? HAHAHAHA!*

Me:	*What do you mean?*
Class:	*You're saying it wrong. It's "pome-granate". Can't you speak English? Are you dumb?*
Me:	*But that's how my mum says it. Pom-mang-granate.*
Class:	*That's the dumbest thing we've ever heard anyone say. You should go teach your mum how to say it.*

Everyone's head whipped round and all eyes were on you as you stuttered your way through the unfortunate and embarrassing situation. What was there to say? You came home, fuming and self-conscious, and looked up the spelling. Of course it was "pomegranate"! How could your parents have got it so wrong? You said "pom-e-granate" one hundred times, until you were certain it would come out right the next time you had to say it.

Let's not pretend that pronouncing "pomegranate" as "pom-mang-granate" is the only questionable thing your Sri Lankan parents do. Their own traditions and traits live on through you – whether you like it or not – and these aren't always easy to explain to people who don't understand. Especially when there's no one around who looks like you, eats like you or lives like you. Sometimes it feels as if no one is backing your corner.

If people don't get it, you try to explain. Or you just put up with it. Everyone says your hair is greasy, but they don't realize it just has coconut oil in it to make it healthier. You have to ignore people at school laughing at your very full eyebrows and sideburns, or because your packed lunch smells funny even though it is better than their boring soggy tuna mayo sandwiches. You feel forced to lie to your friends about not being able to hang out in the evenings and weekends to hide that your parents are way stricter than everyone else's. (That last one will go on for a while, by the way.)

Well, fourteen-year-old me, I'll let you into a little secret. Yes, you do learn how to say "pomegranate" out loud correctly. But ten years on, after all that time, you will still always say "pom-mang-granate" in your head first. You can't let it go, even if you want to. Occasionally it slips out when you're with friends, but instead of furiously blaming your parents for your embarrassment, you tell a story about how your ammi and appachchi moved to another country and achieved everything they dreamed of, even though they still say "pom-mang-granate", or tell you to "turn down the light" and "get down from the train". This is, you know, just quirky and endearing and unique.

Yeah, you heard me right. Ten years on and you will figure out that your parents aren't ignorant or embarrassing just because they say a few things differently from everyone else. You'll realize that one (OK, fine, maybe more than one) mispronounced word or phrase is nothing compared with everything else they have achieved in moving to a new country and starting their lives again from scratch. I mean, that's actually a pretty big deal. They moved to another country to put you through one of the most enviable education systems in the world and set you up for the rest of your life. They were even lucky enough to migrate in comfortable circumstances: by choice, as economic migrants. Remember that when they left Sri Lanka, many other Sri Lankans were fleeing for their lives from a deadly civil war. Unlike much of your diaspora, there's so much trauma that you'll never have to see or experience. You're luckier than you currently know.

I know it doesn't seem like that now. Trust me, I get it – I lived through your life too. Being even a bit different is hard at school, and being the child of immigrant parents is especially challenging. You don't realize you have to defend all the weird and wonderful habits you've inherited and practised in the privacy of your home until someone is calling you out on it. And you can't even defend yourself, because it is just who you are. Yes, I do eat rice and

"Being even a bit different is hard at school, and being the child of immigrant parents is especially challenging."

curry with my hands. No, I don't celebrate Christmas and Easter. Yes, I only wash my hair once a week because that's all it needs. I thought that was normal. Don't you do all those things? You don't? Oh, crap.

These little things will probably make you feel different in a bad way and no one wants that. You'll blame your parents for a lot of it, just like you did for mispronouncing "pomegranate". After all, they are meant to teach you how to navigate the big wide world, so what good is it if they are teaching you how to do it in all the wrong ways? This is just one of many mishaps that make you think that all the Sri Lankan things about you are uncool or a burden. You'll try to distance yourself so you're more like everyone else, but please, oh please, don't.

Fine, sneak out, shave your legs and go to art school, but don't pretend to be something you're not.

"Fine, sneak out, shave your legs and go to art school, but don't pretend to be something you're not."

I know, at the moment, you think fitting in is the most important thing (and I promise that all of your friends are feeling that too, not just you), but as you grow older, you'll come to appreciate all those little differences as quirks that make you the person you are. Hang tight and believe in who you are and where you come from. That includes where your parents come from. Don't worry about what everyone else is doing.

On the other side of that, don't compliantly and mindlessly be what your parents want you to be just because it's easier than telling them "sorry, but I don't want to be a doctor" or "yes, I do have a boyfriend". It's a frustrating process, but try to see things from your parents' point of view and learn how to balance that with yours. It'll take negotiation and patience and sacrifice, but you can do a lot of those things without shunning your culture and your identity. If you don't find a balance between who you are and who your culture expects you to be, all it will do is cause an ongoing rift with your parents and make you completely confused about who you are when you are halfway through university.

You'll be pleased to hear that despite the many, many mistakes you'll make, you'll do a decent job at navigating the grown-up world. Through university, work, travel and all the people you meet on the way, you'll slowly learn to appreciate yourself and love the things that make you different. Most importantly, for me, and therefore for you, this will mean embracing and engaging with your long-ignored Sri Lankan identity.

You won't believe it now, but you'll start cooking more Sri Lankan food. You'll go out with a Sri

Lankan boy whose ease in negotiating a British and Tamil identity will make you want to learn how to do the same with your British and Sinhala identity. You'll become involved with an incredibly strong group of people of colour who have been changing the game for people like us. They'll open your eyes to a whole new way of expressing what it means to be a woman of colour. You'll finally collect a small group of South Asian friends who will encourage you to celebrate and get involved with South Asian culture. You'll read books and articles and visit exhibitions that celebrate your culture, your history and your identity. You'll even start to learn how to speak your mother tongue.

But honestly, you'll regret not waking up and smelling the Sri Lankan food sooner. Right now, what makes you different is what makes you the person you are, and it is so much easier to find that person if you can embrace that difference. Where you live and go to school is also full to the brim with so many languages, cultures and traditions, so don't forget to offer others the same courtesy.

"They'll open your eyes to a whole new way of expressing what it means to be a woman of colour."

But what you could learn from your parents about your culture and your background is unparalleled. They are your culture and they are your background. You don't know this yet but when you're twenty-four, your parents will decide to move back to Sri Lanka for good. They'll pack up thirty years of memories and experiences and ship them back to the life they once sacrificed for you. You'll lose your family home, the home-cooked meals Ammi brought to put in your freezer and the freshly cut mangoes Appachchi loves so much.

So, when you do stumble over the word "pomegranate", picture sitting on the living-room floor, ripping the juicy red "pom-mang-granates" out of the off-white husk and squeezing them between your teeth until they pop. Remember the red-stained hands, as you fought for handfuls of the tiny red jewels that reminded you of being home in Sri Lanka. Take joy in waking up early to go to temple in east London, getting lost in the folds of the gentle chanting and soft-smelling incense. Have fun making brightly coloured Vesak lanterns in April to celebrate Sinhala New Year and savouring the small eats that Ammi wakes up early to make. Better yet, wake up early and make them with her.

I don't want to turn this into a to-do list, but I don't want you to miss out on all the wonderful influences around you. I don't want you to waste the time you have to spend with your family. I don't want you to feel embarrassed or conscious that your story isn't the same as everyone else's. I don't want you to regret not getting to know yourself, for yourself, sooner.

So, this is my heads up to you. Your parents are right there, right now: take the time to learn from them while you can. Rinse them of everything they know and love about being Sri Lankan and find your own unique way of knowing and loving Sri Lanka too. Try to find out more about the things that make you different, by asking questions and looking beyond mainstream resources (the Internet is both your best friend and your enemy). I know you're not sentimental, but write stuff down more, take more pictures. That includes taking note of the little home rituals and nuances of being part of an immigrant family, because they are what you'll look to for comfort whenever you get lost.

Oh, and just one final tip. If you ever feel the urge to cut yourself a box fringe – don't do it. Trust me, it won't suit you.

Love,
Samanthi

"I don't want you
          to regret not getting
   to Know yourself,
            for yourself, sooner."

FROM NIGHTCLUB TO A & E

A TALE ABOUT DRUGS

written by

NINA DAHMANI

> *In the space of about 40 minutes she went from being super jittery and hallucinating a bit, to being a rigid convulsing body falling off the bench like some kind of inanimate object. It was the most terrifying night of my life. I thought she was going to die right before my eyes.*
>
> **Facebook message: age 18**

In my first year of university, my friend Lucia came to visit me. It was the first and only time we went clubbing together: just a few hours after arriving in London, she nearly died after taking drugs I gave her. I know that sounds dramatic and scary – it was a dramatic and scary experience – but I'm not sharing this story in judgement of any choices that you might make around drugs. I just want to offer you an insight into how quickly and how badly things can go wrong, whether you're taking them for the first or the fortieth time – and I urge you to enter these situations fully aware of the risks.

Growing up, Lucia and I were good friends; we went to different schools but often met up at weekends. We sometimes drank together at the park, the pub or each other's houses, but our friendship wasn't dependent on

"Just a few hours after arriving in London, she nearly died after taking drugs I gave her."

that. We were close. I knew that she, like me, had dabbled with different drugs, though we'd never tried anything together. After leaving our home town to go to different universities, we'd both started experimenting more, so her visit to London was fuelled by the anticipation of finally – inevitably – having a wild weekend together. Beyond the actual university part, moving to London was an exciting (if slightly daunting) experience: I had a big new city to explore, completely different people around me and endless bars and clubs. I couldn't wait to give Lucia a glimpse into my new life.

She arrived on the Friday evening. We had some drinks in my room in halls, and prepared the MDMA I had left over from the week before. There was a sense of expectation: we were happy to see each other and catch up on many months' worth of gossip, of course, but somewhat distracted by what lay ahead. I'd got used to that feeling of anticipation since going out more; it was partly due to transporting an illegal substance across the city, on the Underground, past the bouncers and into the club – and partly due to the rush I knew I'd feel coursing through my body once it took effect.

We took a little of the off-white powder just before we left, and then a bit more when we arrived at the club around an hour later. MDMA can make you feel wobbly and disoriented while it's kicking in, but very soon after we checked in our coats, Lucia started acting strangely: quiet and unfocused. Something about the way she was behaving was just ... not right.

I took her out to the smoking area, thinking fresh air might help. A group of boys sat down next to us. They were obviously having a good time: laughing, elbowing one another and yelling jokes. Rowdy euphoria oozed out of their wide smiles, and their drinks sloshed out of their cups as they jostled each other. I wondered when our drugs would kick in so we'd be able to feel like that too, and I glanced at Lucia, silently willing her to perk up a bit. The boys leaned over to ask how we were doing. I chatted to them for a little while before noticing that, next to me, Lucia had started moving erratically, shaking her head and muttering to herself. Despite being a warm and talkative person normally, she wasn't making eye contact or engaging with us at all. I looked at her, confused and concerned, and she turned to me and snapped, "I'm fine. It's always like this at the beginning." The boys laughed, unfazed by her odd behaviour. We weren't out of place taking drugs here; the bass-heavy, energetic music was a strong indicator (for us, at least) that illegal substances would be

"Lucia had started moving erratically, shaking her head and muttering to herself."

floating around. But Lucia was already on a different level from anyone else in the club.

The banter from the boys turned to light concern when they realized I'd begun to panic. Lucia wouldn't talk to me or respond to my questions and she seemed to be completely off in her own jittery world. One of the boys offered to get her some water – MDMA raises your body temperature and can make you dehydrated. Another tried to reassure me that I was overreacting, saying she just had too much energy from the drugs and I should take her inside to dance it off. Another told me to take her home if I was really that worried. We were discussing Lucia as if she wasn't there – and she wasn't, not really.

MDMA affects your expression, your movements and your general behaviour; it can make you happy and chatty, but it's not a pretty drug (if such a thing even exists). By now, Lucia looked absolutely possessed. Her face was blank, her eyes so wide they could have been bolted open, and her jaw was chattering at a million miles an hour, completely out of her control. Her whole body was trembling violently; she semi-acknowledged the plastic cup of water that the boy came back with, but was unable to hold it, and when I held it up to her lips she shook her head suddenly and knocked it all down herself. We watched her gesturing to imaginary people, turning jumpily this way and that way to engage with the hallucinations, and reaching out into thin air to grab things that weren't there. Her speech, not directed at us – or anyone – was quick and garbled, like when you fast-forward the television. I was in pieces; I didn't know what to do. A part of me worried that maybe I was overreacting like that boy had said – I'd taken the MDMA too, of course, so maybe I wasn't in my right mind. But I knew deep down that something was really wrong. She'd gone too rapidly from being fun and silly to plain scary. I stared at her for what felt like a lifetime, weighing up whether I needed to call a bouncer.

Suddenly, in a tiny voice, barely audible, Lucia whimpered, "I'm slipping..." This was the first thing she'd said that made any sense, so we snapped to attention. Eyes wide open, Lucia slid clumsily, confusedly, off the bench – and then started convulsing on the floor. I grabbed the boy next to me and screamed into his face to get help. He nodded, already scrambling to his feet, and ran off into the darkness of the club.

"I knew deep down that something was really wrong."

The following twelve hours were terrifying and draining. It all went by either too fast or too slow:

the arrival of the bouncers, them carrying her stiff body on their shoulders through the maze of the club, battling with interfering strangers, waiting for the ambulance, Lucia laid out on the cold pavement, the journey to the hospital, her incoherent moans in the ambulance, and the dark, solitary waiting room that they put me in. It was hideous. Each time I try to focus on writing exactly what happened, I simply can't. But she survived. You wouldn't have guessed that outcome if you'd been there.

They put Lucia into an induced coma, and she had to stay in intensive care for a while after. I went to visit her after a couple of days; she was physically weak, but appeared chirpy – for a few minutes, at least. I felt a huge rush of relief when I saw her, followed by a painful knot deep in my stomach when I saw the bruising on her body, her chapped lips, her strained movements and all the tubes going in and out of her. I couldn't even imagine where all the bruises had come from. She smiled weakly at me. We spoke briefly, not really about the night, though she did say she couldn't remember a lot of it. Learning this felt like being punched in the chest – and hard. Naively, I had thought she would remember the whole ordeal. It wasn't like I'd been expecting to cosy up on the end of her hospital bed for a good, juicy debrief like after a normal night out – of course not. But for some reason, I'd expected her to remember. In reality, I'm glad she doesn't have access to the memories I still carry, or indeed her personal ones, but when she said that, I suddenly felt very, very alone.

Lucia tired quickly and her mum offered to walk me out of the hospital. I felt awkward and sad and strange – we didn't speak. There were lots of words tumbling around in my head that I couldn't quite get out: *I'm sorry, are you OK? I'm glad she's OK; can I visit again? Would you want me to? Would she? Sorry, sorry, sorry.* Finally, we reached the foyer. Lucia's mum turned to me, looked me in the eye, and said, "We don't blame you." I remember holding in my breath for too long, steeling myself for the twist. But it didn't come.

"We know Lucia likes to experiment," came next. They were just grateful I'd called someone in time. Apparently Lucia's body temperature had been so high that if the ambulance had arrived just a little later, she likely would have died.

I'm not including this last detail to "congratulate" myself for finally having the sense (and capability, despite the MDMA) to scream for help. The point

"I'm sorry, are you OK? I'm glad she's OK; can I visit again? Would you want me to? Would she? Sorry, sorry, sorry."

I simply want to make is that the stakes are really, really high if you take class A drugs – and not only because they're illegal. Drugs, unlike people, do not discriminate, and you can never know for certain what you are putting in your body or how it might affect you. The worst physical effects that I experienced after that night were headaches, weakness in my body and a lack of appetite for a couple of days. For Lucia, however, the exact same MDMA caused her temperature to skyrocket, her lungs to fill with fluid and her liver and kidneys to be badly damaged.

While the drugs might look the same, there's no guarantee that they're from the same batch – and certainly there's no guarantee that any batch is safe. And although you might know the person who gives them to you, it's unlikely you'll know anyone else in the supply chain. Drugs pass through lots of different hands before they are dealt to consumers, and harmful chemicals can be added in. You are running the risk of death every single time you take drugs.

You don't need me to lecture you about this. I'm sure you've sat through the same PSHE lessons that I did, filled with news clips about overdoses. We all know that drugs have the potential to wreck people's lives. But what you don't learn in PSHE is just how unremarkable taking drugs can sometimes be. Teachers and parents often worry about "the wrong crowd", but in my experience it isn't always as simple as that. I know lots of people who take drugs regularly at weekends and have their lives together again by Monday morning. They are not "druggies" in the way you might expect. Even some of the most unlikely people at my school tried or still take drugs in some way. For a few, it started out of genuine curiosity about how you might be able to bend your mind, or see the world differently. Honestly, for my first time, it was just because it was available, and looked fun. Not peer pressure, just that my peers had it. And after I'd done it once, it became easier to do it again. Drug-taking shouldn't dictate your friendships, just as your friends shouldn't dictate whether you take drugs. Some of my good friends find the idea of drugs revolting or just totally uninteresting. Some of them have tried things, others haven't. It really doesn't matter: what is important is that we are friends, despite our lifestyle choices.

Chances are at some point you will be faced with a choice about whether you want to try one drug or another. If you choose (and it should always be *your* choice – not your friend's or anyone else's) to enter into this kind of high-risk situation, one thing I advise you to do is to think about all the worst possible outcomes and how you might deal with them. It might not be the done thing to take a moment to mull over death at pre-drinks, but it's worth it. Equally important is considering how the people you're with might react if something bad were to happen to you: even if they have your best interests at heart when they're sober, will they be capable of calling for help when they're intoxicated? Additionally, you need to be aware that if you're all taking the same batch, you could suffer different effects, like me and Lucia – or all suffer adverse effects. Never be too proud to tell someone if you feel you need medical assistance, or be too scared to seek help on behalf of someone else, even if you're not totally sure they need it. Why take that risk? Time spent (understandably) worrying about the

"Never be too proud to tell someone if you feel you need medical assistance, or be too scared to seek help on behalf of someone else."

"Whatever choices you make, please make sure they are your choices."

police, what your friends or parents might think, or whether you're overreacting, could be crucial minutes wasted in saving someone's life.

Lucia was eventually discharged and we met up quite soon after the incident, as she had to come back to London for a follow-up hospital visit. I remember feeling sick, nervous, ashamed and awkward, but Lucia was her normal lovely self. Over the next three years of university there were no more attempts at partying together, but we saw each other occasionally when we were back at home for holidays and kept in touch with messages during term time. Like many friendships, however, ours slowly dissipated. We haven't spoken for a couple of years now. It's a shame, but I think it happened naturally and gradually, and not so soon after the incident that it could be blamed solely on that.

Despite that harrowing night (and the many anxious, restless nights that immediately followed), I've taken drugs since. I still like to go out to clubs and stay up till the next day. I know that some people will find this baffling, ignorant, disrespectful and the rest. I get it. But every time, it is my choice and my risk. What I have learned from my experience, though, is to be hyper-vigilant in looking out for adverse effects in myself, my friends and strangers around us when we're out – and the importance of trying to be prepared for a life-threatening situation. At the very least, I am now completely aware that I'm entering into one. Of course Lucia and I knew the risks, but they felt abstract. Neither of us could have guessed that our night would end like that.

Whatever choices you make, please make sure they are your choices. When you're caught up in the moment, it can be all too easy to forget that drugs are illegal and highly dangerous. Despite what our parents might want to believe, talk of buying and trying drugs happens among lots of different people, from lots of different backgrounds and school social groups. And although many people, young and old, will have an opinion on the matter, one thing that often gets left out of the conversation is what to do in an emergency. I hope this story will have demonstrated that the best – the only – thing to do in that situation is to seek help. Whatever regrets you may have after a night out, potentially saving a life will not be one of them.

some names have been changed, including that of the author

"YOU SPEAK WELL FOR A BLACK GIRL"

BLACK IS WHO YOU ARE

written by

NIELLAH ARBOINE

School was decent. Went over to see Nina after school and on the way the Year 9 "fan club" just got at it! "Look at you, er, what's up with her hair?!" I mean seriously, you can never win and you try not to take it to heart and I don't, but I don't know what I'm doing wrong.

Diary entry: age 16

Dear Niellah,

I'm about to turn twenty-five and you're sixteen. When I found this entry in my diary, I thought back to those years at school and that feeling of not fitting in – not to mention the hideous grey polo necks. It made me want to write to you to tell you that you are doing just fine. Trust me, you are. And I promise you that one thing you must never worry about is your blackness. Black is who you are; it's not about what you wear, the music you listen to or how you speak.

You've grown up in south London, and in your secondary school are kids from all walks of life. Mostly you enjoy school. You play the French horn in orchestra and brass ensemble and you sing in the choir and the chamber choir. You're the sarcastic joker in your friendship group and people are drawn to your dry humour. It's fair to say you are a bit of nerd and you sometimes find books more interesting than people. There's something so satisfying about getting lost in a story. But you can't shake the feeling that to some people, you are the wrong type of black.

I want to talk to you about this, Niellah, because it's making you too anxious to sleep and you keep writing about it. There are some girls, two years below you, who always laugh at you. They are black, like you, but they're more Just Do It bags and Kickers, while your mum is dead set on you having socially repulsive Clarks shoes and a sensibly large bag for your textbooks. These Year 9 girls scoff at you on the bus and in the school corridors, mainly when you are by yourself. You believe they are laughing at you because of your hair, your choice of clothes and the fact you're dragging around a massive suitcase-sized musical instrument while listening to David Bowie on repeat. You worry that these girls think you aren't black enough.

I want to reach back through time and hug you. You haven't done anything wrong, so you mustn't blame yourself. I know it is draining trying to avoid those girls all the time. And yes, I could tell you to ignore them and not take it to heart, but it's OK to be upset. Nobody likes being laughed at or whispered about. Of course you feel awful and embarrassed.

It's confusing too: all of you are black but you don't understand one another. These girls are making you feel lost. A million unanswered questions are whirling around your head. Is it possible for you to be an Oreo: somehow black on the outside but white on the inside? Is that supposed to be a compliment? How can you act white if there's a black face looking back at you in the mirror? Are you somehow failing at being black? Are you not being your true self?

This letter is to tell you to be proud of who you are. You come from a long line of amazing people from Jamaica, with a vast, rich history that your mother has made sure you know about. Do you know what it has taken for you to be here today? What your ancestors have survived so you can walk this earth? You are the only person who gets to define your blackness.

What you are discovering is that some people have a fixed idea of what it means to be black, and if you don't fit their expectation of blackness, you are doing the whole thing wrong. For those girls at school, black means dressing in a certain way. But to be honest, to be black you just have to be black. Wild, right? So don't change what you wear just because those girls laugh at your leg warmers. If you want to wear them over your tights with your dolly shoes, then you do just that. Wear them with pride, wear them for practicality, wear them because you want to! Right now, you are spending your time at school trying to fit in, but you will spend the rest of your life trying to stand out. (And, you

"You are the only person who gets to define your blackness."

never know, you might see those same girls waltzing around in leg warmers soon.)

I know you also feel that your blackness is defined by the music you listen to. At school, and in society at large, knowing the words to every rap song supposedly makes you black. And while it is a part of black culture for some, it doesn't have to be for you. It's OK to have an eclectic taste in music and listen to soul, pop and glam rock. Some of what you are listening to right now is categorically just bad, but that's a different point and if it makes you feel good, it doesn't matter.

Fall wildly in love with David Bowie while everyone else listens to what's popular in the charts. Bowie's music will grow with you. You've been enthralled by him since you saw him strutting around with his spiked blond locks in *Labyrinth*. When you heard "Rock 'n' Roll Suicide" for the first time it knocked the wind out of your lungs. It's a little odd that a black girl growing up in the noughties feels so close to this white superstar born in the forties. But maybe you're not that different. You were born and raised in the same south London neighbourhood after all. Perhaps you walked the same streets.

You don't yet understand that black musicians have influenced so many different genres of music. R & B, hip hop and grime are the obvious ones, but there's also jazz, ska and rock 'n' roll. You've only ever seen skinny limp-haired white guys in rock bands, but soon you'll discover that Big Mama Thornton, Chuck Berry and Sister Rosetta Tharpe paved the way for the Elvises of the world. Blues and rock 'n' roll were invented by African Americans and there's a whole scene of alternative music that is for, by and about black people just like us.

Don't forget how lucky you are to play so many instruments, even if it feels like a social repellent at the moment. Your mum made sure you were always in those lessons, starting with piano, recorder and violin in primary school, and then the French horn in secondary school. You're a music scholar – be proud of that! I know hauling that massive instrument case onto the number 39 bus is a headache, but how many people do you know who can play the French horn? It isn't going to make you prom queen, but don't let wanting to fit in stop you from doing something you love.

Please don't worry about being seen as the wrong type of black at school. Wear what you want and listen to whatever makes you smile. But be true to yourself. I want you to make your own choices: choices that will make you happy. I'm worried that you are reacting to those girls by trying too hard to fit in with your white peers and the white world around you. Your teachers certainly think you are the "right kind of black". You've even been told you speak well for a black girl. Try not to take this too personally, but that isn't actually a compliment. If you're being told

"Don't let wanting to fit in

stop you from doing

something you love."

you look nice, talk eloquently or act differently for a black girl, the implication is that black people can't do or be any of those things.

Yes, you just want to be accepted. Yes, the norm in our society is whiteness. So I understand why at the moment you feel that being compared to whiteness is a good thing. But really it insinuates that there's something wrong with being black. It is offensive and demeaning. You are not better than any other black person because you play the French horn or listen to Bowie. Such comments say more about the speaker's prejudices and basic preconceptions of blackness than they do about you. There is nothing wrong with being black and there's no right way to be black. Existing is enough.

You certainly don't have to be a model minority to fit in. Check in with yourself, Niellah. I'm sure you've bragged about being one sixteenth Asian, as if somehow just having a black lineage wasn't good enough. I know you're a bit embarrassed by your many names and the neighbourhood you grew up in. Are you rejecting parts of your culture to assimilate? You avoid bringing in food from home in case people ask questions. And what about your bedroom walls? They are littered with photos of gaunt white women in *Vogue*. Where are the women you can see yourself in? People that look like you, with your hair and your shaped nose and your colour eyes. You mustn't avoid things associated with your blackness just to fit into someone else's ideology.

Your Afro hair is one thing that's obviously part of your black identity and at the moment you have a problem with it. You are obsessively straightening it, even though it is burning and breaking off at the ends. I understand you're only doing this because you want to fit in with beauty standards you see around you, but it's a rigged game. Those standards are always going to be unattainable to you, no matter how much you straighten or dye your hair. Believe me, your stiff spiky bob isn't any cuter than your soft kinky curls. However much you pretend your fringe is intentional, your hair is actually just damaged. Learn about protective hairstyles and care for your locks. Your natural hair is beautiful: look after it.

Be happy in your blackness. It's a long journey and you won't stop trying to figure stuff out. It's hard to love yourself when the world keeps fighting against

"There is nothing wrong with being black and there's no right way to be black. Existing is enough."

you. Being invisible, yet always seen, is a difficult line to walk. You mustn't pit yourself against your peers; I'm sure you and those girls at school have more in common than you realize. But don't get swayed into believing you're the only black girl to like certain things or speak in a certain way, as if that makes you special or different. You're not the first black person to like rock or classical music; you're not the world's only black nerd. You're most certainly not the first black person to wear leg warmers.

Instead find solace and strength in your black friends and family. Keep reading too. It will open doors and help you through your whole life. But maybe try reading books with characters who look like you. Be the centre of your own story. Find musicians who sing the genres you love, join groups for blerds (black nerds) and fill your room with beautiful art. Listen to the advice of the people who love you, like your mum: she's always fighting for you to see the beauty in your blackness. And keep writing that diary. Write down every encounter with your crushes, but also use your diary as a way to be honest with yourself. You never know where it might take you!

I know I've come across as quite demanding, but it's because you mean the world to me and I want the best for you. You're going to have to learn to love

"Be the centre of

every black inch of yourself. It's not easy and maybe you'll spend your whole life trying, but you are worth the fight. I have faith in you. There is no right way to be black: our differences make us beautiful and we must value them. But first you have to love the skin you're in.

Love,
Niellah

your own story."

MY VIRGINITY AND MY CHOICE

DATING AS A BRITISH MUSLIM

written by

SARA JAFARI

My mind is so conflicted. Guy is everything I should want in a boyfriend – he fits the bill for all the characters I've created in my fantasies, but I find it hard to believe we will last long. Then there is the issue of sex. My body is totally fighting it and to tell him the truth would be mortifying. I'm half considering breaking things off to save myself the embarrassment. But I'm always going to have this problem. And because he's popular, I'm scared that if I tell him, other people will find out that I'm a virgin. Not that it's a bad thing, but it's seen that way when you are nineteen years old. I just can't face telling him. I had a dream I did and it was terrible.

And anyway I have this fear that doing it will send me to hell. Or bring shame or regret. And going this long without having done it means I can't even just go and do it with someone as if it means nothing. But even if I could, I know I wouldn't want to.

Diary entry: age 19

Dear Sara,

You're spiralling as you write that diary entry. Pause. Take a deep breath. Try a nice hot bath – even seven years later, it's still the easiest way to calm down. You're nineteen, you've left home where your parents carefully monitored you, and you've started university in London. Adjusting to this change isn't easy. At home you weren't allowed to go to parties, and now suddenly you're thrust into a world centred on socializing and nights out (as well as studying). It's an exciting time, but remember to take care of yourself. Worry less about what people think of you: what you think about you is much more important.

You've never been a fully practising Muslim and your faith is something you still struggle with, although you believe in Allah and being a good person. But it's only now that you've moved away and can do whatever you want, including talking to the opposite sex, that you've realized how much your family's beliefs in the importance of virginity and purity have shaped you. Particular rules were enforced upon you by your parents to keep you "pure". You hated this. You wanted to be "normal", go to sleepovers and chat to boys like your friends did. Of course there has never, ever been any question of you having

"You've realized how much your family's beliefs in the importance of virginity and purity have shaped you."

sex outside marriage. You hate the idea of virginity being a "gift" you bestow on another person (it's really not – your body is not something that can be "gifted"). You've always argued with your parents that women are not objects to be kept shiny and new until marriage. But now, away from them, when finally you have the freedom to do what you want, deep down you are wondering if you should be kept shiny and new after all.

You've always been a hopeless romantic, waiting to be swept off your feet. Case in point, when describing in your diary a new-found crush on a boy at university, let's call him Guy, you say "he fits the bill for all the characters I've created". Summer holidays were often spent churning through fantasy YA romance novels. One of the happiest moments of your childhood was reading the Twilight Saga. Maybe it's because Edward Cullen is every Muslim girl's fantasy: he's hot, forbidden and wants to wait until marriage to have sex. (OK, maybe he's just yours, I don't know!) The last point is important, and rare. For years you've imagined what it would be like to have your first boyfriend and what dates you'd go on, but you've recoiled from any chance of these things happening – even a kiss – because that would mean confronting questions about your virginity. You'd rather bury your head in the sand.

"Edward Cullen is every
            Muslim girl's fantasy:
    he's hot, forbidden and
                    wants to wait until marriage
                            to have sex."

But now, as you write that diary entry, you are finally forced to confront your fears. You've somehow found yourself in a relationship.

Not much has changed between then and now, except Instagram is currently all the rage instead of Facebook. It is Facebook where Guy first messages you. You were Facebook friends without having talked in person before, but you were in lectures together. It took you liking one of his pictures to capture his attention. You hit it off – unexpectedly because you've always been a bit weird-looking and no one ever fancied you at school. But he likes your vampy style, which is surprising as he seems the type to only date white cheerleaders. People who find out you're talking comment to your face that you don't seem his "type", muttering something about you being Asian, and him being "him". In a sense, this shock that he could ever like you makes you like him more – which is probably your first mistake, Sara. You're so easily influenced by other people. But you do find that you both have writing in common and a similar sense of humour. He writes you long Facebook messages, and it's the first time you feel the fluttery, weightless feeling in your stomach. You can't look at the messages straight away because you feel a mixture of excitement and fear.

When you speak in person at a house party, having already messaged each other for a week prior, he goes over to you and says, "I have a confession to make." That's when you feel your heart pounding – a fight or flight instinct – because the look in his eyes tells you what he's

"He writes you long Facebook messages, and it's the first time you feel the fluttery, weightless feeling in your stomach."

going to say. You could run, as you always do, but instead you say, "And what's that?"

"I fancy you," he says, before asking for your number. It's not quite the suave or mysterious dialogue of the boys in the books you love, but it's real.

What follows is a string of fanciful, thoughtful dates with Guy. Trips to the V&A, walks through Nunhead Cemetery (in hindsight it's a weird place for a date, but you seem to like it). You even have your own coffee shop that you call "your place". You have your first ever kiss (but he doesn't know it's your first, because that's something you're embarrassed about – but don't need to be). Everything seems to be going great.

But all the while you're ignoring the questions of a) your virginity, and b) your faith. You haven't told him – or anyone apart from close friends – that you are a virgin because it suddenly seems like everyone lost their virginity between the ages of fifteen and eighteen and you were the only one left. Another thing you are embarrassed about.

And what makes it more confusing is that, despite the excitement of being with Guy, you don't want to lose your virginity. You aren't sure how to explain that to anyone eloquently, so you keep it to yourself, letting your thoughts fester.

Now, this is important: you can enjoy kissing

someone, love their company, find them unbelievably attractive and *still* not want to have sex with them. This is about knowing and trusting how you feel, even if it's not your first time, even if you've had sex with the person before in the past. That tight feeling in the pit of your stomach, that feeling that it's wrong – listen to that. That's your gut telling you something. Listen. You should never do anything if it doesn't feel right or you feel pressured, and you absolutely shouldn't feel embarrassed or ashamed to say no.

You have embarked on this relationship without really thinking about what you will do when sex comes up. Increasingly, as is apparent from the diary entry, you'll begin to develop the fear that losing your virginity will send you to hell. Or it will be something you'll regret for the rest of your life. A few months into dating Guy, you will finally muster up the courage to tell him you're a virgin and you need to take things slow. But really, honestly, you're biding your time because you actually, deep down, have no intention of having sex with him. Somewhere, you know this won't last. And he'll hug you and say, "Of course", and how understanding he is will seem sweet. That is, until he makes an increasing number of offhand

"You should never do anything if it doesn't feel right or you feel pressured, and you absolutely shouldn't feel embarrassed or ashamed to say no."

comments about how horny he is. About how long it has been since he last had sex. Sara, this is a red flag – it is possible to keep it in your pants without getting red-faced and annoyed about it. It's a tactic, pure and simple.

The pressure will soon feel too much. You might have thought telling him would have made it easier, would have lessened your anxiety, but you'll soon begin to feel like you owe him something for all the dates he's taken you on. His side comments will become more frequent, and it will become clear how important he believes his needs are, while he never once asks about yours. Another red flag. You deserve someone who cares about and respects you enough to ask about your background and why you feel the way you do.

So, following some passive-aggressive text messages that you'll instigate in a panic, you'll break up. It will only be a four-month relationship, if you can call it that, but it will shape you. It will be the moment you realize how complex your relationship with sex and virginity is. And how, without knowing it, the rules you've grown up with have embedded themselves in your brain.

Next time make sure you confront your feelings, your faith, and get comfortable with yourself *before* you enter a relationship, not during. It will save you heartache and be so much better for your mental health, trust me.

Despite Guy's charming disposition, your gut will be right. In the year after you break up his true colours will be shown and you'll learn that you made the right decision. Perhaps, even, the feeling in your gut will be Allah guiding you.

Even now it's difficult, as a supposed British Muslim, to write this letter. You are always going to feel like you don't have the right to call yourself a Muslim for engaging in such a relationship. And you also feel guilty, sometimes, that you still don't see that relationship as wrong. You'll find there are conflicting sides to being a British Muslim – from wanting to please your family and stay true to your faith, but also wanting to be happy and do what you want to do. Sara, I know it can be isolating trying to navigate sex, because it feels like you have no one to talk to, no one who can truly understand why you think the way you do. You'll resort to googling whether having a boyfriend is wrong (and you'll continue to google all your problems as you get older with mixed results). Muslim forums say you will go straight to hell for kissing him (reassuring, thank you!) and when you confide in atheist friends, they tell you to "just do it, who cares!" (also not very helpful!).

You will worry about how your mum will judge you if she ever finds out about Guy. You think she'll

"Even now it's difficult, as a supposed

love you less, perhaps even dislike you. Rest assured, Sara, with age you will be able to talk more frankly with her, even ask for her advice about boys (honestly, I'm being serious; I was flabbergasted too) – and she won't hate you; if anything your bond and understanding of each other will become stronger.

The anxiety that comes with being a British Muslim will never completely go away, for you anyway. It will always feel like you're running around in a computer game trying to reach the next level but are unable to find the door to let you out, while the villain is slowly encroaching upon you. But things have changed since you were a teenager. There are new platforms out there (such as gal-dem) where you can read stories about girls with similar issues all around the world. When you wrote that diary entry, you didn't know anyone in your predicament, so you just winged it while simultaneously worrying yourself to oblivion. Shared experience is important. Use the resources you have. Tell your story, if you want. Or read the stories of others. And I'm sure you'll find you're not alone.

The one thing I want you to know is that it's OK to be confused about sex. It's OK to wait until marriage. Or you might not want to wait and that's OK too. It's OK to say yes to one person but no to another if that is what feels right for you. You might not know what you

British Muslim, to write this letter."

want to do, and you can – and should – take the time to think it through. However it may feel now, you don't have to lose your virginity by a certain age. None of it is embarrassing, not really – and that's something that you need to get out of your head. So often our actions are judged, especially as women. If you have sex in your early teens you risk being called a "slut"; if you abstain from sex until your twenties, or thirties, you are a "prude". If you wait until marriage people will say, "But that means you've only had sex with one person!" It's time people stopped focusing on other people's bodies, on other people's choices, and focused on themselves. So listen to your body and your mind, and don't be too hard on yourself.

And, Sara, one day you will meet someone who will wait – or maybe you'll decide you no longer want to. That I'll leave for you to find out.

Love,

Sara

some names have been changed

"However it may feel now, you don't have to lose your virginity by a certain age."

MY COUSIN MEDYAÏ

OUR STORY

written by

KUCHENGA

Growing up, everything around me confirmed my ugliness. People of colour were conspicuous by their absence. They weren't in the books from the library I wolfed down or the TV series I loved. True beauty was pale skin turned tan on the beach in *Neighbours* or on the California coast in *Baywatch*. Everyone agreed that these women defined beauty, and all I wanted was to be beautiful. In a home video when I was very little, I can be seen with my younger sister running around our flat in Tottenham with towels on our heads. We're pretending our hair flowed graciously, instead of sprouting upwards defiantly. Even then, I did low-key kinda know that it was a warped fantasy to pretend to be white. Yet, if anyone had cared to ask, I would have told them what I really wanted was to be a girl.

I marched through childhood in an alien boy's body that I had become resigned to but not comfortable with. I played with the girls. I wore girls' clothes. I paid attention to gender and was dedicated to femininity in a very serious way. The adults around me found it amusing until I got to primary school, where they felt I should have grown out of these odd quirks. My mind wasn't catching on to the supposedly natural order of things and it was time for me to masculinize. The boys in my class would always ask why

"I marched through childhood in an alien boy's body that I had become resigned to but not comfortable with."

I wanted to play with the dolls. I would ignore their questions because as yet I had no answer.

When I was six years old and in Year 1, I begged my parents for a doll in front of their friends, to their intense embarrassment. Aunty Sonia (not my aunty, but called so out of respect and cultural practice) gave me one of her daughter's old dolls. I felt fulfilled when I held her in my lap. She had such full cheeks and a rotund body that felt solid and unchanging. I combed her auburn hair all evening until it shone. I wanted to look after that doll with such care and consideration. I wanted to give that doll the precious protection that I had not grown up with. But she disappeared before I even had a chance to name her. Anything that I loved, that was deemed too girly, would be cruelly removed without explanation. In this world, neither I nor what I loved was safe.

I gave my mind permission to be elsewhere and I lived in other worlds quite easily. By the end of primary school, I was just too weird for anyone to take seriously. I was lonely. My father had gone back to live in Zimbabwe for a period and my mother was working all the hours God could send. I lived in a house of women: my mother, my sister and me. I dreamed that one day I would travel the world as an air stewardess, but I couldn't tell anyone. If I were to explain my longing to be a beautiful, lithe woman, wearing red lipstick with a little hat perched jauntily on blow-dried hair, I would be laughed at. Telling anyone my dreams, while in the body of a boy, was too impossible. Until she came along...

"She came out of nowhere and yet it was like she had always been there."

My cousin Medyaï started walking to school with me one day, heading towards the W3 bus stop in Northumberland Park. She wore a ribbed olive green turtleneck, a tartan felt miniskirt, olive-green tights and brown loafers. She came out of nowhere and yet it was like she had always been there. She was the daughter of my Uncle Ransford in Jamaica, who had had a love affair with a white Canadian woman. We were both ten years old, born days apart in September, but had never met because my cousin had been living between Toronto, Montreal and Paris, where she had trained at a dance school since she was a child.

The two dots above the ï announced her as exotic and melodic: MEDYAÏ [*meh-dee-eye*]. Her name was the perfect accompaniment to the percussive force of my name: KUCHENGA [*koo-chen-gah*]. People loved saying our musical names together: "Have you seen

Medyaï and Kuchenga?" Or "Are Kuchenga and Medyaï coming?" Suddenly I had a cousin and a champion at my side.

Medyaï looked you in the eye. She ate homophobic fools for breakfast and was confident in her intelligence. Everyone wanted to be around her, and from her I drew strength, confidence and power. She had an answer for everything. The ugly black queer duckling now had a beautiful light-skinned cousin. We were two Dora Milaje warriors, straight out of *Black Panther*, but in a distinctly urban setting. Every pavement we walked down became a runway and we were the definition of "sass". Our auras, combined, made us invincible.

I wore boys' clothes, but I tried to style them like the tomboys of the nineties. Baggy jeans and combat jeans were de rigueur for both genders and I was in love with Aaliyah and the girls from All Saints, but to try wearing anything explicitly *femme* was crazily dangerous. The most radical thing I could do was grow out my 4C Afro. But it was Medyaï's 3C hair that was marvelled at for its softness and versatility. She could straighten it without relaxer *whispers* just like a white girl. If it rained and the curls came back she wouldn't run. She would stand in the rain and laugh. Her loveliness could weather all conditions.

"She would stand in the rain and laugh. Her loveliness could weather all conditions."

With her caramel complexion, she was the first light-skinned black person who stood up for me in the face of colourism. She would dismiss the hierarchy of shade when other black people mocked my broad nose, thick lips and dark skin as too African. She wasn't just woke, she was awake with eyes wide open, looking for offence. Medyaï shielded me as if it made her feel good, as if it were an honour. She loved me.

Everything I wasn't allowed to do, Medyaï made OK. For years I would go to Covent Garden and watch the dancers in Pineapple Studios through the window from the street outside. I would collect the pastel pink and yellow leaflet with the classes to show my mother, who would just look at it with a mix of disinterest and distaste. But then Medyaï came along and I was allowed to dance. We loved the choreographer Alvin Ailey and made plans to go and see his work in New York. Behind closed doors, before my parents arrived home, she gave me permission to be me.

But even with Medyaï in my life, despair and struggle still permeated my dreams:

I find myself falling into some sort of lake. I grab on to the side of a cliff and try to pull myself up. I do so, but when I reach the top I can't get my legs to push me over the edge. There is a fence behind it. Not very strong, just yards of holey green mesh held up by sticks. I try to pull myself up by holding on to it.

Diary entry: age 13

I had panic attacks in the middle of the night and I would wake up in the early morning paralysed and unable to breathe. Once I started breathing again, I had to read. I read *The Color Purple* in one delicious night and decided I could probably survive. I began to dare to dream. I spent my dinner money on fashion and music magazines: copies of *Glamour, Vogue, Vanity Fair, Elle, Vibe, Essence* were held to my breast as I twiddled across the playground. I knew I was going places. No one else around us could see the point of reading about lives that were not our own. Even my bullies couldn't bring themselves to touch the glossy pages of those magazines that breathed femininity.

In secondary school I took to learning French like a duck to water. My Zimbabwean father chose not to teach us his mother tongue of Shona, and I had always felt bereft that I was not bilingual. Medyaï spoke French, and the allure of a shared, secret language was hard to resist. The elegance of French appealed to me. It felt like a language for languid tongues and bodies that knew how to recline, stride and pose. There was a promise that in Paris I could find a certain kind of *liberté*. In the early mornings I would creep down the stairs to watch French Open University programmes. In a dark room, with the milky electric glare from the television, I lived in a matrix where a different tongue told me that some day I would have access to glamour. One morning immediately after this programme, a documentary came on about Stella McCartney and her time at Chloé. Just as it was coming to an end my father stomped in. He turned off the television and whipped around to hiss: "No wonder everyone calls you gay."

This was not wholly inaccurate. My bullies were sinking their teeth into a language that would become their daily chants: "batty boy" and "chi chi man" and "Why are you so gay?" At this time, I was most definitely boy-crazy, as all my girlfriends, including Medyaï, were. I had a difficult love affair with a boy called Bunny, and there were so many other boys I spent the whole time thinking about. But Medyaï was the only one who thought it was completely normal that I was obsessed with boys, fashion, literature and psychology. The older we got, the more people would make acidic jokes about anyone who was not straight. Medyaï would not stand for it. She knew herself to be comfortably bisexual and was unafraid to be the lone voice standing up for all LGBT people. She never swerved in her conviction that we deserved to be left alone but preferably loved.

I went to the mixed sixth form at Camden School for Girls, and learned about the suffragettes and feminism. There was no violence in this small haven of education. Walking along the top floor corridor at the end of my second week, the sun poured in on the polished parquet floors and I realized I was safe.

"She knew herself to be comfortably bisexual and was unafraid to be the lone voice standing up for all LGBT people."

It couldn't have been more different from my secondary school: there was no boy around the corner who would grope me, punch me or slap my bum. I could start blossoming. My difference was celebrated and valued. I campaigned to become a senior prefect and threw sweets into the crowd of younger girls at assembly. I felt comfortable enough to start wearing tighter clothes, head wraps, fur coats and lip glosses. I got on the androgyny train and found a tailcoat that Marlene Dietrich would have worn. The morning of Founder's Day, when I became head boy, I walked into the hall to give my speech. The hall was bedecked with white and purple flowers with dark green stems: the suffragette colours. Tentatively, I had begun my journey to finding myself.

By the time I finished sixth form, my parents had lost their long battle to masculinize me, and homelessness followed. In a hostel in west London, I met my first trans girls, Jamie and Emmanuelle. Medyaï was living in north London and had been doing well modelling. She and I slipped into a new life that was at first exciting and then dangerous. We began to exist in a chaotic spiral where we were never sober. Our lives were about raves, parties and

> **"Tentatively, I had begun my journey to finding myself."**

substances. But it was evident that, in this life, we were going the way of Icarus. The sun was getting hotter and hotter and our wings were starting to burn.

I moved from London to Paris to Brighton to Martinique and back again. I was running to find love anywhere it had been vaguely promised. But I would never find it, and I would return with my heart broken and the woman in me suffocating. Then came two tragedies: my mother got Alzheimer's and Medyaï began to fade away. After a life that had sparkled with such vivacity, Medyaï died quite unremarkably. A drug overdose. I lost the best friend I had ever had. My spiral became more desperate. I was spinning down into a cave where I was more alone than I had ever been. In this cave I spoke with the many that had gone before me. I received a message in Medyaï's voice: "You're a woman. Transition."

I was not scared. I knew I had to try. I am now three years sober from everything. I live a life that's beyond my wildest dreams filled with an attainable and sensible amount of glamour. I live the life of the woman I'd always imagined but never thought I could realize. My body feels right. I move through each day smoothly. I am in constant contact with a group of incredibly successful women who are my closest friends. Together we dare to be bold, brash

'You're a woman. Transition.'"

and vulnerable together. I'm a writer and a journalist and my work lives on platforms for *Harper's Bazaar* and *Vogue*. I take myself on dates to the cinema and theatre and museums, so I can really drink in the experience without interruption. I love being the mysterious woman who does not need anyone. I look people directly in the eye when I speak to them because I have the protection of my community and my ancestors.

I have a lot of love in my life. But when there wasn't love, I had Medyaï. In a way, Medyaï has become an ancestor. She died but she is always with me. I changed my middle name to hers by deed poll. But I took off the umlaut. So my name is now Ms Kuchenga Medyai Shenjé. Because there will only ever be one Medyaï, and I know that the woman I am today would never have made it without her.

some names have been changed

"I look people directly in the eye when I speak to them because I have the protection of my community and my ancestors."

MY BOYFRIEND BOX

THE ART OF

BREAKING UP

written by

LAYALE

After every break-up, I have a ritual. I throw away or delete all traces of that relationship. Photos, text messages, scrapbooks and jumpers – everything. It cleanses the soul far better than chocolate or crying. But I do keep one thing: a love letter from each boyfriend, written in the scruffy cursive of a boy between the ages of fifteen and twenty-three. And to each letter I attach a list detailing why exactly we broke up. I keep these letters because I think somewhere, between the cringeworthy lines and heart-wrenching memories, there are lessons to be learned about love. Some people read Rupi Kaur after a break-up. I read love letters from old flames.

I'll be honest: I hate being single. Being single means takeaways for one, and no one wants to be that sad loser eating a kebab (OK, let's be honest, two kebabs) in bed on a Sunday watching TV alone. But when I look back through the letters and break-up lists in my boyfriend box and remember those feelings of love lost, validation and rejection, I'm glad that however nostalgic I might feel, I haven't yet settled for someone who isn't right for me. I am still figuring out all of this. So if you've come here looking for answers on love and relationships, my boyfriend box is unlikely to be helpful. But if you're searching for something that shows how love is

"Some people read Rupi Kaur after a break-up. I read love letters from old flames."

messy, complicated, funny and sometimes just plain crap, then I suggest you get some ice cream or two kebabs (not both – that's gross) and buckle up – it's a bumpy ride.

Let's start with the first boy I ever fancied. There's no letter in the boyfriend box, though – you need an actual boyfriend for that.

> **Name: Laith (or Nice Eyes)**
> **Age: 16**
> **Song: "Otherside", Red Hot Chili Peppers**
> **Reason for break-up: We were never actually together**

Do you remember the first boy you ever fancied? Like, properly fancied, couldn't-stop-thinking-about-him- thought-your-life-would-end-if-he-wasn't-in-it fancied? I do. The setting was perfect: an Islamic summer camp. That meant gender-segregated dorms, night-time curfews and a horde of sexually frustrated Muslim teenagers. I was thirteen; Nice Eyes was sixteen. I was wearing a headscarf, had braces on my teeth and had zero sense of style. He had bad acne, olive skin and piercingly beautiful blue eyes. A group of us snuck out and climbed onto the roof. We talked about Red Hot Chili Peppers and he told me to listen to "Otherside". I nicknamed him Nice Eyes (imaginative, I know) and "Otherside" became the top-played song on my iPod Classic (yes, back in those days).

After camp, I obsessed over Nice Eyes and his dreamy blue eyes. Two years later, my wish to see him again was finally granted. I was going back to summer camp and, through my diligent investigative skills, I learned from his sister that Nice Eyes was going to be there. This time I made sure I looked hot.

I wore a skin-tight dress (over jeans, of course, to keep it modest), my headscarf backwards in a turban style, an inch of make-up and large hooped earrings. I was ready for the love of my life.

The moment came. Those dreamy blue eyes were just as I remembered. His acne was significantly worse. He said hi. I almost died.

And that was it. For the next five days he barely spoke to me. The moment that I had been playing over and over in my head – that he would take one look at the new, hotter me, fall head over heels and instantly profess his love – never happened. In fact, I've never seen Nice Eyes since that summer (or found him on social media).

While I didn't technically break up with Nice Eyes – I don't think you can break up with someone whom you were only with in your head – my break-up ritual began to take shape. I also learned a very valuable lesson. Sometimes, however much you may wish otherwise, they're just not that into you, even when you're at peak hotness. Harsh, but true.

At this very same camp, Nice Eyes had a less hot, dorkier cousin. So I decided to mend my broken heart by flirting outrageously with the next best thing. Introducing actual boyfriend number one: Haaris.

Name: Haaris
Age: 16
Song: "Cecilia", Simon & Garfunkel
Reason for break-up: My GCSEs

At camp, Haaris would pass me notes in class and text me from the gender-segregated dorms. I was rebelling against my parents' conservative religiousness, and his attention came at a pivotal moment in my adolescence when I realized I was a) hot and b) not very religious at all. By day we learned Qur'anic Arabic and by night we made out in the bushes behind the school.

After camp, we began a long-distance relationship between Sheffield and Liverpool. He would send me soppy notes detailing our love. This is the one that made it into the boyfriend box. It's about the first time he saw me and it's gross. (I apologize in advance.)

When I saw you at the recent course... You were so beautiful ... lyk stunning. I'd lose my appetite in the food hall sometimes from getting butterflies. I lost a lot of sleep on the first night thinking about you. I never would've conjured the thought that we'd be in each other's arms 2 nights later... =) yumyumyumyum hehe!

Haaris was the first boy I explored my body with. He came to visit me at the weekends. I'd lie that I was seeing a Muslim (girl)friend to my parents and then sneak away with my new boyfriend. We would make out wherever we could: in parks, cafés or pubs if we could get served. We were shameless and it was both disgusting (for spectators) and amazing (for me).

One time my parents were out of town for the evening and Haaris came round (tip: never, ever do this; it's not worth the stress or fear). I let him explore me with his hands and tongue. He asked if I orgasmed. My response was, "What's that?"

After that, I was determined to figure out my own body. The first thing I did was hold up a mirror to my vagina. I had never seen it before. I discovered there was a lot of information out there: videos, diagrams, TV shows, books. I had one goal over the next few months: make myself orgasm. It took a while, but after much patience, relaxation and exploring what turned me on, I got there. Knowing what works and feels good for you is far more important (and useful) than any amount of snogging on a park bench.

While I was figuring all this out, I was also revising for my GCSEs and starting to think about my A levels. I knew one thing for sure: I was going to go to a good university and no one was going to stop me. Haaris began to feel more like a distraction than anything else.

While I liked having someone to message and discuss with my friends, I was frustrated by things he said and did. I realized I liked the idea of having a boyfriend far more than I liked my actual boyfriend.

But should we break up? I dealt with my indecision by writing lists. This is my fifteen-year-old self's guide to spotting the end of a relationship, finishing it and getting over it.

Why we should break up

1. Talks about himself constantly
2. No Valentine's gift
3. Hard to keep convo going
4. Going into moods constantly
5. Jealous

How to break up

1. Really like you – been awesome BUT
2. Ultimately completely different people
3. Not going anywhere long-term
4. I've got a really important year – very serious about doing well
5. Nothing to do with you; it's ME

What to do after break-up

There are lots of other things more deserving of your time.
This is NOT worth ruining your GCSEs.

1. Read a book!
2. Stop texting in English class – you need to focus
3. Do ART. Your art GCSE is in a MONTH
4. Hang out with friends – make more of an effort
5. Start going swimming
6. Start an exercise class
7. Deactivate Facebook
8. Order university prospectuses
9. Clean your room and KEEP IT CLEAN
10. WORK HARD – it'll be useful in the long run
11. Perfect guitar

(The last one may have been slightly ambitious but hey, gotta aim high.)

Eight years on and these lists are still pretty badass. It's hard to break up with someone. You never really know if you're doing the right thing. Haaris might not have been the love of my life, but I did like (maybe even love) him. And at the time it was hard to see how I could find someone else whom I could be that silly and strange with, and whom I could be so open, vulnerable and honest around. It felt like it would be so much work to have to build all of that up again.

All you can do is trust your gut. Deep down, when I wrote those lists, I must have known there would be someone more compatible with me. I broke up with Haaris and in the first two weeks of being single watched six seasons of *TOWIE*. By the end I had no regrets. And now I'm so glad I didn't settle for the first boy who walked into my life.

Instead I focused on my exams, became a French fanatic and found boyfriend number two: Pierre.

> **"All you can do is trust your gut."**

Name: Pierre
Age: 17
Song: "You Are My Sunshine", Nat King Cole
Reason for break-up: I went to university

This was the year of my A levels. I had moved from *TOWIE* to Truffaut. I memorized quotes from French movies. I thought of myself as a mini Audrey Tautou and couldn't wait to go to France on a summer holiday.

I went to a little remote village and I met Pierre at a village party. I was sick on his shoes. He kissed me despite my vomit breath. A week-long holiday romance ensued.

When I returned to England, Pierre went to Cuba. He sent me a postcard. It was the first postcard I'd received from a boy and it felt so adult. It was also written entirely in French. I think it's in my boyfriend box mainly because I was so happy I could understand it.

Coucou mon amour. J'ai pensé que tu aimerais que je te rapporte un petit cadeau de Cuba, alors voilà ce que j'ai trouvé de mieux, j'espère que tu apprécieras (si tu ne les aimes pas tant pis, "c'est l'intention qui compte").

Translation: *Hiya my love. I thought that you would like it if I brought you back a little present from Cuba, so here you go, this is the best I could find, I hope you appreciate it (if you don't, no worries, "it's the thought that counts").*

Pierre and I started a long-distance relationship. We spoke on the phone, Skyped and WhatsApped for seven months before we saw each other again.

"I introduced him to the basic concepts of feminism; he introduced me to French swear words."

I introduced him to the basic concepts of feminism; he introduced me to French swear words. He was the perfect form of A level revision in many ways, although sometimes I wonder how much more work I would have done had I not spent most of my evenings Snapchatting him.

It made sense that I went out with Pierre. I wasn't allowed to party, and long distance meant that my parents were unlikely to find out. And I was still determined to do well at school. As most of our chat took place online rather than IRL, it meant I was in control of the time we spent together.

When he finally came to England, I was eighteen and we knew that we were going to have sex. We knew because we had spent so long talking about it. I knew his reservations, excitement and fears and he knew mine. I had also spoken to my older sisters and friends about their experiences of sex. I didn't feel alone, nothing felt taboo and I felt safe.

We were also very prepared. We had lube by

the gallon, and I had started on the contraceptive pill the month before. While many friends described their experiences of sex as anticlimactic, I'd say it was less of a let-down and more of a relief that it could only get better from here (and boy, did it get better).

I have a lot to thank Pierre for. He made me feel awesome when most of my friends were dating snotty-nosed boys in our school who made them feel like crap. He was funny and weird and kind and utterly head over heels.

But unfortunately for him, I didn't get an A* in my French oral exam. From then on our relationship spiralled. My relationship with the French language was tense, and in turn my relationship with French men was wavering. Amidst rage at my parents, listening to Laura Marling, learning guitar and reading Voltaire, I wrote lists about everything I was going to achieve at university away from my conservative Muslim home. Pierre didn't feature in those lists.

My next two relationships took me through my university years. It was here that I realized I had been pretty shielded from the world and those break-up lists didn't match reality. I thought folk music, guitar playing and reading French philosophy were cool. (Apparently they're not?!) I was also suddenly surrounded by a lot of people who were very different from me – namely posh people who oozed entitlement.

Consequently my next two boyfriends were quite obviously a result of my growing confusion about who I wanted to be. The first one, Joe, was, on paper, perfect. He was a guitar player, and he loved poetry and books and theatre. But he was also posh and white and wasn't raised in a strict Muslim home. We were too different. His boyfriend box letter is full of stanzas like "the Rolex on your wrist, cursed gold, will tear you down from Lego Babels, down to lonely patios". With Joe I felt unwanted, undesired and stupid. As a rule, if they claim they're a poet, run a mile. I'm kidding – #notallpoets.

The next (and most recent) boyfriend, we'll call him Dean, seemed cool in the way most people define cool at university. He loved to party and drink too much. He listened to techno and wore bucket hats. With him, I felt part of a crowd I'd always thought I wanted to be part of, doing things I saw as far cooler, trendier and edgier than things I had done without him. (I conveniently overlooked the time when he and his friends dressed up as "chavs" for a party, or the time his friends said they "just didn't fancy black girls".) But actually I was already pretty cool – I was a published writer, an avid reader, a political activist – I just didn't believe it. At twenty-three, I finally realized that coolness is subjective – and I cared more about dinners and books than I did about drum and bass.

Since coming out of these relationships I have been spending time figuring myself out, nourishing my friendships, dating too much, eating kebabs and, of course, writing messy lists. My current list starts with two words repeatedly underlined:

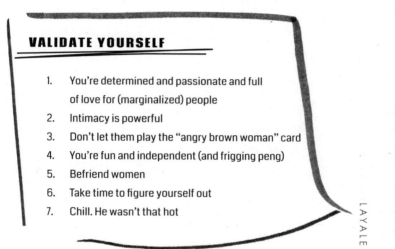

VALIDATE YOURSELF

1. You're determined and passionate and full of love for (marginalized) people
2. Intimacy is powerful
3. Don't let them play the "angry brown woman" card
4. You're fun and independent (and frigging peng)
5. Befriend women
6. Take time to figure yourself out
7. Chill. He wasn't that hot

There is no rule book for relationships. The more break-ups I go through, the more lists and letters I add to my boyfriend box, the more I learn that it's not too much to ask for a hot, woke, funny, weird and interesting person who adores you for who you are. And while my relationships are unique, there are some takeaways from these four that I think we can all share. I will display them to you in my favourite format:

1. Don't rely on someone else for your self-esteem
2. Keep your own hobbies
3. Be careful with people's hearts
4. You are infinitely more beautiful than you think you are
5. Boys come and go
6. Don't call them
7. You owe no one your time
8. Nourish your friendships
9. If they've hurt you, don't take them back
10. Let yourself cry
11. Know your own body
12. Never bail on your friends for a boy
13. Block them from social media
14. Listen to your gut
15. Be vulnerable
16. Say no
17. Cherish being on your own
18. Delete their number
19. Listen to your friends
20. Set your own boundaries
21. Give yourself time
22. Be unapologetic
23. Stop watching *Bridget Jones*
24. Chill out on the kebabs
25. Write lists
26. And never settle

some names have been changed, including that of the author

"It's not too much to ask for a hot, woke, funny, weird and interesting person who adores you for who you are."

"WI LIKKLE BUT WI TALLAWAH"

YOU ARE STRONG BECAUSE YOUR VOICE ALWAYS MATTERS

written by

LEAH COWAN

I was thirteen when Britain and America invaded Iraq in the spring of 2003. Iraq was thousands of miles away from my small town in the West Midlands, but the anger surrounding the invasion changed the way I saw the world. As the conflict unfolded, I discovered just how easily my voice could be silenced if I didn't join with others to shout loudly about injustice.

From reading the newspaper headlines in my local corner shop and watching the news with my parents, I learned that Tony Blair, the UK's prime minister, and the American president, George W. Bush, were claiming that the president of Iraq, Saddam Hussein, was stockpiling a hoard of weapons, known as weapons of mass destruction (WMDs). Blair and Bush used this as a reason to invade Iraq. In the end, no such weapons were ever discovered.

If you had asked me before the invasion if I was interested in politics, I would have rolled my eyes and written a comment about you in my lockable diary. At thirteen, I thought politics was something that happened to other people. The word conjured up images of men in suits arguing with one another on the green leather benches of the Houses of Parliament. But the invasion of Iraq pushed me to start asking questions about things I hadn't thought about before. Why was one country allowed to drop bombs on another country? Was democracy supposed to be so violent?

I wasn't the only person with questions: all over the world huge protests erupted in response to the proposed invasion of Iraq. I watched on TV as millions took to the streets, waving placards with fiery rage in their eyes. I thought I understood the principles of democracy: that it was about fairness and ensuring that all citizens' voices were heard. So when Blair and Bush announced that the invasion would go ahead, despite the marching and chanting and anger, it became clear to me that the people in power are very good at talking and giving speeches, but don't always listen. The shouts of the protesters – people who saw a connection between themselves and the people in Iraq who would have their lives torn apart by conflict – were ultimately ignored by the men in charge of two of the world's most powerful countries.

The day of the invasion, 20 March 2003, was a Thursday. As I walked into school, nibbling on a Cheestring, I remember feeling a palpable buzz in the air. Everyone was talking about Iraq. At morning break, my friend told me there was going to be a protest at lunchtime and we would run out of school. I didn't believe her: our town seemed so disconnected from the shouting crowds protesting in city

"People in power are very good at talking and giving speeches, but don't always listen."

squares and the shining tanks rolling into Baghdad, the capital city of Iraq. Sure enough, lunchtime came around and there was no sign of anything resembling the protests I'd seen on the news.

But as the bell rang to mark the end of lunch, suddenly it happened. Instead of piling into the corridors and heading to afternoon lessons, everyone spilled out into the playground, chattering loudly. A boy from Year 11 shouted something and, without warning, students started running away from the school. The gates were unlocked and we streamed out onto the road. We were like a flock of birds, one moment flitting about in the sky, and the next, swarming together and taking shape as a unified force, a single action.

The deputy head raced to the gates. He announced that we were not allowed to leave school under any circumstance. He told us that the head would make a statement outside his office at

"By coming together and using our voices,

8.30 a.m. the next day. As single students we could be easily pacified. But by coming together and using our voices, just for a moment, we tipped the balance of power. Nevertheless, unsure of what would happen if we stayed outside, most of us gradually trickled back into school and the day carried on as normal.

The next morning, I joined a smaller crowd of students gathered outside the head's office. I'm not sure what I hoped the head would say, but I wasn't expecting to be told that the protest was nothing to do with Iraq but "just another excuse to truant".

just for a moment, we tipped the balance of power."

These were words I had heard other teachers exchanging the previous day, but I didn't expect them to come from his lips, with such disdain for us. Anger rose inside me as I realized the head couldn't imagine a world where we might have an opinion worth listening to or any kind of political agency. He just wanted school to continue as normal. So like Blair and Bush, he silenced our concerns in favour of his own interests. I can see in the poem I wrote in my diary that evening that I was full of rage and disappointment. I had followed the rules and my voice had been silenced.

20 March 2003

War. God.
All around me, my world,
Is smashed to pieces.
Blair, Bush, Hussein.
A 2-sided triangle of hatred.
3 silly boys playing at God.
"Just another excuse," they say
To truant.
For some, it's true.
But all the others, we care.
People will die.
Civilians.
Like you and me.
Our last chance for peace
Just slipped through the fingers of hope
And was shattered by conflict.

Poem: age 13

For some of us, the protest may well have been a reason to truant, but given the school had an exclusion rate of one in twelve, I don't think students were hanging around looking for "excuses" to skip lessons. Apathy hung thick over the school like a cloud; we destroyed the things that were given to us. Our teachers were too busy breaking up fights and dodging projectiles to think about nurturing our politics. The protest was an act of pure rebellion, not necessarily motivated by my classmates' feelings about the invasion, but an attempt to have our voices heard, on this issue or any, in a world which seemed to care very little for our perspective.

I learned something important that day. By trying to dampen our resistance, the head achieved the opposite: he revealed that his power was strengthened if we played by the rules. In that moment, I saw that if we raise our voices against authority figures that have misused our trust and respect, we can start to shake the foundations of their power. On the day of the Iraq invasion, I backed down and returned to school. I wonder what would have happened if we had persisted with the protest?

"If we raise our voices against authority figures that have misused our trust and respect, we can start to shake the foundations of their power."

When I look back, I can see that this day nudged me onto a path of questioning everything I thought I knew about politics. Any trust I had for people purely on the basis of their position of authority evaporated.

I started to realize that politics was something I lived and breathed. It was something I was aware of every time the police pulled my dad's car over for no reason, which never seemed to happen to my white friends' parents. Now getting to know my history felt like a small internal revolution. My family, like all families, shared a politics which grew out of a fertile soil of stories passed down through generations. Our grandparents told us tales of migration from Jamaica to Britain in the 1950s, and of perseverance and hard work, cleaning houses as children before school to make ends meet. My parents discussed the Ban the Bomb marches they had joined in the 1970s, and my mum showed me her Campaign for Nuclear Disarmament (CND) peace symbol pin badge. These stories helped me understand my place in the world: how we got here, and the struggles we had faced along the way. Power, race, class and gender were no longer abstract concepts but the very lifeblood of

"Power, race, class and gender were no longer abstract concepts but the very lifeblood of my daily existence."

my daily existence – these precious family histories tangled up in my DNA.

The Iraq War continued for eight long years, during which time I finished school and went to university. I wanted to work in solidarity with people whose voices had been silenced by the British government, so I became involved in a grass-roots group called SOAS Detainee Support (SDS) that supports people locked up in immigration detention centres. These centres are used to hold people while they wait to find out whether they are allowed to remain in the UK, or if they are going to be deported by plane to another country. Often the people locked up are fleeing from torture, abuse or conflict. The centres are largely modelled on high-security prisons and the detainees can be kept waiting years for a decision to be made. There is no proper healthcare or Internet access, the food is poor quality and family visits are restricted. I believe this is unjust and unfair, and at SDS I tried to offer support in a practical way. I helped those seeking asylum to gather evidence for their claims, found translators for legal documents and pestered slow-moving lawyers.

It is important to push back against injustices wherever we see them, as a step towards creating the world we want to live in. You have a voice, and justice and freedom are too important to leave in the hands of people who do not listen to you. I'd encourage you to think about the issues that matter to you and how you might speak up for them. If you struggle to be heard because you have been muted by other people's expectations of what you have to say, know that your voice matters. Joining a protest with others who share your passion and conviction for change can feel like the exact counterpoint to the helplessness imposed by the incredible power of the state stacked against you. At Yarl's Wood Immigration Removal Centre, a predominantly women's immigration centre in Bedford, I joined a protest where we flew balloons and kites in the sky so the women detained inside could see our messages of support. I've joined marches on the streets to lift up the names of Sarah Reed, Sean Rigg, Mark Duggan and Rashan Charles, black women and men who have died at the hands of the police or in prisons in this country.

Protesting is valuable, but not an end goal. We're not under any illusion that we can just sign a petition or go on a march about climate change and then kick back with a bowl of popcorn and watch the ozone layer stitch itself back together. Our generation is opening up space for more inclusive ways of resisting huge global forces. We must continue to centre the voices of people who are so often muted and silenced, including people of colour, LGBT people,

"Your voice matters."

undocumented people, working-class people, disabled people, sex workers and indigenous people.

Your dreams of a fairer world might look different from mine, so I can't tell you exactly how to use your voice. However, there are some things I wish I'd known the day I wrote that poem in my diary. Most importantly: you are more powerful than you think. In Jamaica we have a saying that goes "wi likkle but wi tallawah". It warns against underestimating someone who appears small and weak but in fact is strong. Your strength is not defined by someone else, on their terms. Anger and protest are strengths. Softness, compassion and finding peace are strengths. Writing in a diary is strength: this type of strength reinforces you, and sends you back out into the world with fresh energy and new ideas. Who knows what your strength feels like and where it will lead you.

Do not expect the powerful to use their power to make the world a better place – there are enough history books documenting that there is little precedent for this. Instead find the stories and people who inspire you. For me, it is women like Nanny of the Maroons, who was part of a resistance community that escaped slavery on plantations in Jamaica in the eighteenth century and fought back against the British oppressors. I am inspired by Olive Morris, a young civil rights activist who set up resistance and empowerment groups for black women in the UK in the 1970s. I read the words of Assata Shakur, a member of a black revolutionary group who struggled against police brutality and racism. In 1977, after a trial which her lawyer described as a "legal lynching", she was put in prison for allegedly killing a US state trooper. In her autobiography she describes being beaten and tortured while incarcerated. We must speak the names of these people, whether we shout them like a curse or whisper them like an incantation, because most history books do not tell our stories.

You can be an agent of change and address inequality in any number of ways. A single conversation with a friend or relative, if it feels safe, to explain an issue that you care about can have a huge ripple effect. If you organize with other people as a collective like Nanny, Olive and Assata did, your plans and actions will flourish and grow, thanks to different perspectives and a wider range of skill sets. Don't let fear hold you back and do not be afraid to bring your experiences to the table as expertise. You don't need a degree or a title to have knowledge. This advice has helped me to do things I would never have imagined back when I was reading newspaper headlines as

"Don't let fear hold you back."

a thirteen-year-old: I've addressed the Trades Union Congress, spoken in Parliament and given a TEDx Talk about inequality.

Many years after that day in 2003 standing outside the head's office, I read an essay by feminist writer and activist Audre Lorde, in which she states: "the master's tools will never dismantle the master's house". This crystallized what I learned that day: playing by the rules of people in power will never achieve radical change. Sometimes we have to seize change where we can, with our own hands. Perhaps this, too, will be your life's work.

FIND YOUR SUPERPOWER

YOU'RE THE ONE AND ONLY YOU

written by

CANDACE
LEE CAMACHO

It's very early in the morning of Picture Day in fourth grade. I'm ten and on my tippy toes. Quietly I creep into the bathroom to shave my moustache. No one can know, especially Mommy. She'd be upset but I don't know why: all I want is for my friends to know and remember a beautiful version of me. I run Mommy's pink razor through the water before it hits my skin.

No one at home can know I'm shaving my moustache, but when I get to school I want everyone to see. Gabby is the first to notice. We're neighbours in computer lab and she mentions that I seem different. "It's my moustache!" I respond with pride. "I shaved it this morning." She comes closer. "Ah! Yes, that's it! You look much better!"

The auditorium is a football stadium of friends when we sit for our class photo. I'm happy to fit in. My Afro is short and delicious. I pose in a bright yellow blouse. The day feels like a kiss on the cheek.

Mommy picks me up from school and I have to share my elation. I want to tell her I fixed the problem before she had to worry. "Do you notice anything different about me ... maybe about my ... facial hair?" The car halts like a bitten tongue. Her look pierces through me, my seat, the car itself, perhaps all the traffic behind us too. My mother is a mountain, with a hurricane in her throat.

I was not allowed to shave again.

With big bug eyes and hair all over my body, I went through life feeling like an unfortunate combination of many ugly things. I was the only girl in school with a moustache, and it made me invisible and the centre of attention all at once. I was constantly forgotten, purposely ignored or bullied excessively by my classmates or cousins. Beneath my awkwardness was an overflowing feeling of embarrassment and shame. Why was I born like this?

"I was the only girl in school with a moustache, and it made me invisible and the centre of attention all at once."

Hair in funny places was just the beginning of my struggle with my body. At fourteen, it seemed that even my pimples had pimples. I smelled no matter how much floral deodorant I put on. My new boobs were large, with long stretch marks from growing so quickly, and already sagging from ill-fitting bras. I felt like an alien on the wrong planet. Wearing baggy clothes became an everyday survival tool and I often dressed like a tomboy. I didn't always feel like a girl so I hid my curves and legs. I was so aware of my unloveliness and my paranoia bloomed into very low self-esteem.

Television and movies made it worse. I didn't see myself in many characters and it was obvious they'd never create a princess with a moustache, although we clearly existed. The girls I saw on TV all had a similar look, one I could never get close to. When Hilary, Miley and Selena sang about their insecurities, I never completely believed them. Did they really have my problems? I developed an unhealthy relationship with celebrity. Straight hair, a small body and light skin became the blueprint for beauty that I held too close. My mind was filled with dangerous ideas of what "normal" should be.

The first social media profile I made was on Myspace, where you could design a website, connect with your classmates and upload photos. My friends would constantly post cute pics and selfies while I barely wanted to show my face. I felt like I couldn't share anything without editing the photo or completely covering my mouth to hide my gap teeth, big lips and wild facial hair. My online presence turned into a performance. Online became a place where I could modify, control and manipulate the images that represented me. I made myself seem more confident by taking photos from certain angles, using filters and Photoshop. But it wasn't real at all.

Straightening my hair was another attempt at shape-shifting. My older cousins were already

"Online became a place where I could modify, control and manipulate the images that represented me."

trading their gorgeous locks for relaxed hair, synthetic wigs and extensions. I began to straighten my army of curls each day, but it only buried me deeper beneath my sorrow. I damaged my Afro and burned my scalp, sometimes leaving scabs on my forehead. I tried experimenting with make-up too. Early on a school morning I'd slide thick strokes of eyeliner on, hoping it would help in some way. I was determined to fit into the world I saw, at any cost.

There was tension between who I was and what I was pretending to be. Consciously and subconsciously I was associating being ugly with my race and culture. I wished I wasn't black because I saw the care and praise white girls got so easily and I wanted the same treatment. Why was it hard to love prickly and chubby me? I tried to understand my feelings by writing haikus in my diary:

i am small. strawberry
lips rumble to God
who can hear my tears dry?

tangled hair a ball
of thoughts yarn spaghetti that
does not stop growing

bushy furry girl
big bulging eyes kept to herself
protect her heart

Poem: age 14

Over time, this darkness grew into a deep anxiety where my mind would play tricks on me. I began harming myself, and sometimes I would try to scratch off all my skin. I did not care for my body in any way. I stopped showering because I thought it wouldn't make a difference. My smile became yellow like I had mini sunflower petals for teeth. When my period came, I hardly changed the pad. I collected items on my bed: clothing, books, garbage, homework, shoes, food, plates, wrappers, cups, forks ... everything and anything, in a huge stack. I would force myself to sleep on top of the dirty pile. My mom would beg me to clean and I'd completely ignore her. I was punishing and neglecting myself with little desire or hope of changing the situation.

Every day I prayed to feel less, because my feelings were building up at a pace I couldn't contain. Rage swam in my chest. I did not know how to communicate or to release the pain, and I felt lonely and voiceless. At one point, I asked God to either end my life or come down and fix me. I didn't share my feelings because I was trying to swallow them. But keeping everything inside was a huge mistake. I should have asked for help. I was unwell and I needed support.

I'm glad I'm still here, with the opportunity to tell you my story. If you ever think of harming yourself or feel life is not worth it, you must speak to an adult that you trust immediately. I know it is hard to ask for help when you feel that you are "other", out on the margins, different from the things you see online and in magazines. But only by asking for help will you discover there is no such thing as "normal". There is more than one way to exist.

The Internet is an endless place where you can get lost in comparing yourself to others or creating a facade. It is all too easy to stare at photos and wish you look like someone else. Or to post something that isn't true to your real feelings. I hope you're not using technology as an opportunity to put yourself down like I've done in the past. What you see online shouldn't define how you feel about your body. Social media can be a great tool for staying connected with your friends, but you should never stop seeking out real-life relationships. There's nothing like gathering together with the people you love, who love you for who you are. Eat snacks, play games and let your laughter intertwine.

Social media can be an opportunity to celebrate and document your existence. I am here. I've always been here. I will not be erased. I am beautiful! But tell your own story and don't let anyone tell it for you.

"What you see online shouldn't define how you feel about your body."

No one else is from where you're from, with your exact parents, mind, gift and smile. This is your superpower: you're the one and only you. There is an incredible strength in this simple fact. Be yourself and always feel safe in your body. No one should feel shame for being who they are. Especially if you are non-conforming like me: expressing yourself in a way that does not perfectly fit under "masculine" or "feminine". We must actively include and inspire one another, no matter our various identities.

Up until now, a certain group of people with power got to choose what is worth documenting. That era is ending and it's up to us to make sure it never returns. We must hold on tight to what makes us unique, and celebrate our differences. Let's learn about our histories and preserve the stories of our families. One day I hope to be someone's great-great-grandma. I know you will be whatever you dream. And maybe our great-great-grandchildren will find this book and see that we are on a mission to heal our pain towards their future.

"No one else
is from where
you're from,
with your exact
parents, mind, gift and smile.
This is your superpower:
you're the one
and only you."

LISTEN TO YOUR INNER VOICE

YOUR FIRST GIRL CRUSH WON'T BE YOUR LAST

written by

LIV LITTLE

You are sixteen when you first fall in love with a girl. It is an intoxicating, all-consuming feeling. You have never been particularly shy when it comes to dating, but you've never wanted someone to like you back as much as you want her to.

She is unbelievably beautiful and mysterious. You're desperate to know what she is thinking, but can never quite tell. She's the sort of girl who keeps you on your toes, and you find that fascinating. You fall for her, certain she's the first person in the world who is right for you. Without sounding like a condescending adult, you're being dramatic but that's OK: it is all new and that's how you feel.

You've already had drunken nights where you kissed your close friends at parties, Katy Perry style, during rambunctious games of spin the bottle where the boys were very much in control. But these moments mean nothing in comparison with your feelings now. When you first meet her, you suddenly can't see anyone else. Something clicks into place. You've only ever been close with one queer girl before, so this is unknown territory. It's new and confusing (in a good way) and you're wondering if these feelings are "normal", whatever that may mean. Allow yourself to feel excitement. Don't fear judgement or the girls at school who single out the "lesbians" – they're immature and not worth your attention.

You'll tell your friends that you like this girl. Like really, really like this girl, and the boys will make pathetic jokes about what two girls do together as though your feelings are somehow made up or invalid. Because you aren't taught about relationships outside of heteronormative ones, you may internalize their ignorant comments. Your sex education at school has been limited. Remember that awful time when you had to put a condom on a banana in sex ed? Your headmistress, for some reason, decided it was a good idea for her to deliver this particular session. She reduced sex education to nothing more than a conversation around contraception, STIs and teen pregnancy. You've seen diagrams of vulvas in the context of childbirth, but it hasn't gone much further than that. You are going to have to unlearn what society packages as the norm: that a woman's sexual pleasure is in the hands of a man.

Up until this point, your sexual encounters with boys have been underwhelming at best. Your body has been a vessel for their pleasure as opposed to a vessel for your own. You haven't thought much about what your own sexual pleasure means: when your best friend sat down on your bed and told you about masturbation

"You are going to have to unlearn what society packages as the norm: that a woman's sexual pleasure is in the hands of a man."

you were not only embarrassed but horrified. But sex should feel good and you deserve to figure out what you like. You don't have to sleep with boys just because that is what your friends are doing. You certainly don't have to pretend to enjoy it when you don't. Sex is not your duty; it is not their right. Nor is it only defined by penetration. Sex should feel good, it should be consensual and you should be able to articulate what you want, no matter how awkward that may feel at first. Sexual pleasure is not something to feel shame around.

I am sorry that one of the boys you were intimate with made a stupid comment about the appearance of your vulva. I'm even more sorry that this made you fear the prospect of intimacy with this girl and other women in general. You've always been a bit unsure of whether your vulva is "normal" or "right". She is. Society has ridiculously unrealistic expectations of what women's bodies should be like. The straight girls at your school who make fun of vulvas that aren't neat or tucked in have got their references from porn, just as the boys have. Ignore them. Bodies come in lots of different shapes and sizes, and you are perfect and important as you are.

Despite all these confusing feelings and worries, your relationship with this girl will blossom. You'll chat over MSN, spend hours talking on the phone every night and waste away summer days in the park. You'll kiss for the first time, awkwardly (mainly on your part), in the bathroom of a sweaty club filled with angsty teens with dilated pupils. You'll enjoy the thrill of it all and you'll replay these stolen moments for days, even weeks, after the event, counting down the moments until you see her again.

You'll be so sure of how you feel that one day after school, you'll go to the regular spot with your mates and they'll all be in agreement when they say, "You should definitely tell your mum; she'll be totally cool." So you'll phone your mum, surrounded by a crowd of your friends, and tell her that you have some news. You'll blurt out that there's a girl you really like, and when she tells you that that's totally normal and that you're at the age to experiment, you'll be confused, if not underwhelmed, that her response isn't more dramatic. You're pretty sure this isn't a phase or an "experiment" and, for you, this is your moment of coming out. But be happy that you have a mother who is open and understanding. She's great and will continue to be your number one supporter.

You and this girl, "The One", will end up fizzling out. Many things do when your heads are in different places. It ends messily. Unnecessarily so. You'll look

"Society has ridiculously unrealistic expectations of what women's bodies should be like."

back at your Facebook messages. For this relationship, Facebook was your diary. In one conversation, you're discussing comments made about the both of you by some of the boys you know. At the time, her Formspring account had been inundated with horrible comments about her sexuality (likely by horrible boys). It was as though these comments had opened a can of worms and, due to the anonymity of the Internet, people were pretty ruthless. By the time you return to the conversation, her messages have been deleted, leaving only a stream of your messages to her. It's as though she has never existed.

25 April 2010 19:01
Her:

25 April 2010 19:04
You: this is all my fault cos i should never have said anything to you in the first place cos this whole hype and shit would never have happened shit wouldn't have got said and there wouldn't be complications cos it would all be normal

25 April 2010 19:11
Her:

25 April 2010 19:12
You: and i'm glad these are the only and last examples of your drama

25 April 2010 19:13
Her:

25 April 2010 19:13
You: cos all of it is long

25 April 2010 19:14
Her:

25 April 2010 19:17
You: yeah let's just leave it, wasssss kinda jokes for a while blessssss

25 April 2010 19:22
Her:

25 April 2010 19:23
You: but the status isn't really necessary

25 April 2010 19:24
Her:

25 April 2010 19:25
You: that's not rude, i've just been acting differently since this whole thing...

25 April 2010 19:26
Her:

25 April 2010 19:27
You: you occupied most of what i thought about and now it's back to old liv

Facebook messages: age 16

These messages are pretty dramatic, but that's just your nature. You'll always be the sort of girl who wears her heart on her sleeve (often in a not-so-cool way).

You make light here of going back to being the "old Liv" but you don't have to. The judgement and unsolicited opinions which you both received are a reflection of the people around you: there is nothing "wrong" with you. Going back to the "old Liv" means that after this relationship, you won't allow your feelings for women to resurface for another eight years. You'll decide that this girl crush will be your last. It won't, but the next few years will be challenging as you figure out who you are and where you fit in. Your sexuality and body image are two things of many that you're trying to understand. You're also black and a woman and they bring their own challenges, but you've got this. You're going to be great.

You'll go through relationships with men, some long-term, which will be good but missing something fairly fundamental. For a while you'll think that this is "your problem", and you'll even self-diagnose yourself as asexual. But slowly you will grow brave and listen to what your inner voice is telling you. When you do finally start dating women, you will discover that sex is all about who you are doing it with. You'll slowly unlearn those messages about heteronormative sex. It becomes all about a connection.

Of course, when you start dating women you'll encounter cultural blockages along the way, awkward conversations with certain family members, unwanted attention from the public and even, at times, interrogation from strangers. You'll feel crushed when your grandmother discovers you are in a long-term relationship with another woman and asks, "Do you think that is natural?" That question will replay in your mind for weeks, months and even years after the words leave her mouth. This isn't because you perceive her view to be true, but because there will be moments when it seems as though things would be simpler if you were straight. But your sexuality isn't a choice. What even is "natural" anyway?

Eventually those who matter will be on board. It might take them a while but they will get there. Surprisingly, your grandmother will be one of the first to support you because she loves you. Your dad will simply avoid any mention of it, but that's just your dad. He'd be the same if you were bringing home a boy – the thought of his darling girl with anyone will never be something he'll be comfortable talking about.

"There will be moments when it seems as though things would be simpler if you were straight. But your sexuality isn't a choice."

I wish you didn't have to spend the next eight years figuring out that it's OK to like women. It really is. Even at sixteen, you are who you are and you shouldn't have to compromise on what will make you happy. That which is worthwhile takes effort and you're no stranger when it comes to putting in the work. Invest in your happiness and everything else will follow.

Don't wait eight years to date another woman. Don't think your first has to be your last. Only you can know how you feel. Be the best version of yourself and start speaking your truth.

"Be the best version of yourself and start speaking your truth."

"I HATE YOU!"

LEARNING TO UNDERSTAND MY MUM

written by

KEMI ALEMORU

In the spirit of a diary, I'd like to tell you a secret. One evening, when I was about fourteen, my mum refused to let me go out when I'd already made plans with my friends. I was so angry that I got my blue-inked Parker fountain pen, raced to my parents' wardrobe, and flicked droplets of ink at Mum's clothes, as if the pen was a wand and I was a witch seeking revenge. Neither of my parents noticed, so I've never had to share this memory before. I know it doesn't show me in a very good light: I was immature and irrational. But it reveals how difficult I found my relationship with my mum when I was growing up.

I'm not sure my mum knew just how hard I found things until something happened a few months ago that made my fourteen-year-old self's feelings only too clear. As I now live in London, away from my family home in Manchester, I asked my mum to look for a piece of writing in an old diary to help with an article I was researching. Rather than post the diaries to me, Mum opened the lilac journal emblazoned with doodled flowers, and began to take a photo of each page. To start with, it was exactly what I expected: my diary was full of soul-baring passages about boys, embellished with idle doodles and plenty of underlining. But as the images came through to my WhatsApp, my face began to feel hot. In some entries I referred to my mum as "stupid", "thick" and "evil". Then there was one entry where I called her "decrepit". And they kept coming.

"I've got to tell someone or something," one entry read. "I hate my mum. Yesterday, I said I wished she would die and I don't regret it."

Another: "I HATE HER. I don't even mean like 'oh yeah she called me this and she smacked me'. It's hate like I'd like to throw a lighter at her fat head."

All I could do was pick up the phone and apologize to Mum over and over again. Even I was shocked. Besides, I certainly don't feel like that now. For the next few hours, we spoke candidly about those years in a way we never had when I was growing up. Somehow Mum managed to laugh. "You might have hated me sometimes, but I'm not bothered about what you wrote about me," she said. "I knew I wanted the best for you and I wasn't going to let you forget that." This made me wonder if we'd clashed so much because we had very different ideas of what was "best" for me at fourteen.

My mother is unlike any other person I've ever encountered. Her love for me is so deep that if she doesn't hear from me for a couple of days, she assumes I've died. Only recently she managed to get put through to my desk phone at work by disguising herself as a business-related caller in

"My mother is unlike any other person I've ever encountered."

order to check that I was still breathing. I've been told my whole life that we look the same: that I've inherited her big eyes, the bridge of her nose, her wide smile and her full brows. I share her effervescence, but also her hot temper. We might be mother and daughter, but we still bicker like classmates. Now I live in another city and there is some distance between us; her desire to be the all-seeing eye in my life only causes me mild frustration. As a teen, it was far more intense. Any degree of motherly meddling felt like an outright assault on my human rights. My one aim back then was to fit in, which was made far harder by her policing everything from my social life to my self-image. I could only see her as a barrier to fun, beauty and boys – so it was no surprise we didn't get on.

I was not allowed to shave my legs, pluck my eyebrows or wear make-up (though I slathered on the Maybelline Dream Matte Mousse in secret). Mum had forbidden me from changing my look, but I was desperately trying to feel less like an eyesore at school. My all-girls' Catholic grammar, which I nicknamed "the Convent", was as traditional as they come. You could be seriously punished for rolling your pleated skirt up at the waistband (so it grazed your upper thigh rather than dangling

> **"I could only see her as a barrier to fun, beauty and boys – so it was no surprise we didn't get on."**

dutifully below the knee); hours were spent doing the rosary or attending Mass; and we could only write with fountain pens. It was also a very white school and I stuck out. I seemed to be the first black person that many of the students and teachers had encountered, so everything about me was new, fascinating and different. I didn't want to be different. One diary entry, written in a neon pink pen, shows my self-image had hit rock bottom:

I wish I was pretty like the girls at school, blonde like some actress. Instead I am fat me. Mum even thinks I am ugly. I was trying to get my crap quiff to stay up and didn't want to take her advice so she said:

"Fine, look uglier than you already do!"

So I'm getting plastic surgery when I'm older, then I can forget about her and her poison comments.

Diary entry: age 15

In mid-noughties suburban Manchester, the look was to have an impressively tall quiff with bone straight hair. But no matter how much I begged, my mum wouldn't let me use a chemical straightener.

Now I can see we were both trying to navigate the tricky territory of Eurocentric beauty standards. I was picking up on subtle cues that my blackness was less normal, less desirable, than skinny blonde girls with straight hair. (This was before YouTube vloggers made girls feel cute with their own natural hair.) My only frames of reference were black women with chemically processed hair, and white girls with naturally straight or curly manes. I didn't know it was possible to be proud of my aesthetic, so my actions were motivated by insecurity.

It must have been frustrating for my mum to watch me pick up on society's toxic cues that girls should care about their looks over anything else. On an undated page in 2007, I describe a war of words Mum and I had which ended in her banning me from going to "my bezzie's bday party". This argument arose during an episode of *Junior Mastermind*. My diaries often skim past crucial details, but I can just about gather that Mum had made a comment that I should aim to be on the show myself and I hadn't taken it well.

"It started because she said I'm dumming down," teen Kemi writes. (Interestingly, given the subject of the argument, I've spelled it "dumming" despite the fact my spelling has always been decent because Mum made me do extra spelling tests with her after school.)

"She's stupid as well, thick as hell. Besides Junior Mastermind isn't for kids it's for mutants."

At this point in my life, I'd decided that it wasn't cool to be smart. My main aim was to be desired, and that meant not being too clever, but funny and also kind of a bitch, like the girls I watched on reality TV at the time. YouTube has a round-up of Paris Hilton clips which will show you what I mean. Mum telling me that I belonged on a general knowledge show was akin to the scene in *Mean Girls* when Ms Norbury tells Cady to join the Mathletes. It would be social suicide. Didn't Mum want me to be sexy, ditzy and popular? Apparently not. It's kind of mad that I had such a visceral reaction to someone trying to push me to reach my potential, rather than allowing me to aspire to be some idiot boy's idiot girlfriend.

One way Mum tried to stop me becoming an idiot girlfriend was to give me one of the earliest curfew times in my friendship group. I always got picked up at 9.30 p.m., when the night was still young. Again, this wasn't something I appreciated.

"Didn't Mum want me to be sexy, ditzy and popular?"

KEMI ALEMORU

149

If I was allowed out until 11 on Friday I could get my friends back – everyone is always talking about what happened on Friday and I can't join in. It's knocked my confidence and I feel awkward in social situations. I will never forgive [Mum] for what she's doing. I hate her.

Diary entry: age 15

It didn't seem like it at the time, but those nights were inconsequential. Dozens of us hung out at the park, shopping centre or on the platforms of our local tram station, drinking £3 Cherry Lambrini and "bonding". An extra hour or two would have just meant I'd have been a little more drunk (which would have been harder to hide), or that I'd have longer to avoid revealing my true feelings to a boy I liked but was too awkward to flirt with. I wasn't particularly lucky in love.

It would, of course, have been more worrying if Mum showed zero concern about dropping her daughter off to socialize in darkened corners of Manchester's suburbs or parent-free houses. Small decisions you make as a teenager can steer you on a very different life path. Mum knew only too well that teenage kicks could have a lifetime effect. I suspect that her anxiety about the people I was spending time with was the result of being a teen mother herself. She always made it very clear that she didn't have any regrets and was happy she started her family early, but she would never recommend her path to her adolescent daughters.

My parents had been together since my mum was seventeen, and they had three daughters by the time my mum was twenty-seven. When I was fourteen, they decided to stop screaming at each other, split up and move into separate houses. They were trying to figure out their own lives, and what they decided moulded ours. Dad moved to Salford, where Manchester's MediaCity and the new BBC studios were, into a modern flat that had no trace of me in it. I stayed with Mum, whose hobby during this period was constant prayer. She had been approached by a new church while running and she dragged me along too, waking me up early every weekend. Everyone there was so happy – almost too happy – and I thought Mum was becoming distracted by an unfamiliar religious zeal.

"I think this whole Bible-bashing thing is pathetic," I wrote. "Dad's gone, so has my sister to London, rather than be with Mum, and my other sister is planning to go to university far away soon. I have to stay here."

I can see now that I was terrified of change. I was projecting all of my problems on to Mum, who was my only constant amid the uncertainty. It was easier to blame my insecure friendships on her strict rules and groundings, rather than my terrible friends. And when Dad actually moved out, instead of processing it and looking at both sides, I wrote that Mum didn't deserve to be happy because I didn't feel too ecstatic either.

"I was projecting all of my problems on to Mum, who was my only constant amid the uncertainty."

But when Dad left I began to see a different side to her. She'd always been quite fierce in arguments and carried that same high energy into every day-to-day task. Now she seemed broken, and one day she suddenly burst into tears in the hallway. I don't think I

had ever seen her cry before. I realized she was the only parent I saw every day, and the one who was always looking out for me. Even when I was in a mood, which must have made it feel like a thankless task, she still made sure I had a place that was a home. Despite her own sadness, she was still trying to put me first.

This dark period marked the beginning of my understanding of Mum as a person who wasn't only my mum. She had her own issues, insecurities and relationships that were independent of me. What she wanted was for us to reach our full potential. My mum is not the type to carry someone for nine months, be reminded of that fact every day with permanent stretch marks and then allow that person to sell themselves short. She raised three decent human beings in her teens and twenties, making them ambitious and willing them to be smart. With mature eyes, I see that she wanted more for us than we did for ourselves.

When my parents eventually got back together, it didn't immediately smooth out my relationship with my mum. What improved it was accepting that we were both trying our best to work out who we were and what we should do about it. Neither of us had the answers. But it's much easier if you show those who love you some understanding. Learning to see my mother as a person, rather than my "fat head" oppressor, was one of the greatest gifts of my twenties. My steely prison guard became my friend. My only regret is that if we had talked more honestly at the time, before the diary incident, we could have reached an understanding far sooner. We could have done things differently to help pacify the pain we were both experiencing as we tackled the pressures of womanhood – albeit at different stages. Now, we're both making much more of an effort to talk. And, if I've got a problem, my mum is the first person I ask for advice, because I know that even if I don't agree with her, at least she's walked my path before, and that experience always counts for something.

"With mature eyes, I see that she wanted more for us than we did for ourselves."

MY BODY

LEARNING, FINALLY, TO LOVE WHAT I SEE

written by

KUBA
SHAND-BAPTISTE

We all have insecurities, don't we? Those uncontrollable bouts of dread and embarrassment that barge into our minds like shameless party-crashers. For some, the thought of speaking aloud in front of more than a handful of strangers can be enough to turn them into sweating, spluttering messes. For others, it's how they look – or don't – that makes their lives much more difficult. As a size 18 to 22, chubby all over, black teenage girl, you can guess what mine were. But although we all have things about our bodies that make us feel insecure, nothing people say, and nothing we internalize, can erase the fact that there is more than one way to be beautiful. I'm living that truth, thanks to coming to that realization when I was fifteen. And I don't see any reason why the lessons I learned back then should be confined to my own experiences – we can all take something from the idea that loving yourself can be life-changing.

"Bwoi, Kuba. Yuh gettin' fat – eee?" I had long endured the bluntness of my West Indian relatives, but it wasn't until I reached secondary school that I began to change my behaviour as a result of the way others saw

"There is more than one way to be beautiful."

my body. Ever since I could remember I had hated my prominent back fat and the way my legs looked in jeans, but I had hidden those feelings by pretending to be the fun, unflappable friend who didn't care about how she looked. Then a few years into high school it dawned on me that others found my fat much more offensive than I ever had. And, always the people pleaser, I began to see my body as a burden that I needed to lift from everyone else. Becoming overwhelmed with self-loathing was my way of coping; if I agreed with what people said about the way I looked, maybe they'd like me more.

I remember the first time someone called me fat in a mean way to my face. I was reluctantly strolling back to lessons with classmates after lunch, when one of them, a boy ironically a few sizes bigger than me, compared me to the first fat famous figure he could think of. It wasn't a very inspired insult, and he only said it because I'd one-upped him about some stupid remark he'd made. In response, this boy, let's call him Peter, spat out what was meant to be a scathing insult: "Yeah? Well, you're Fat Monica." And it floored me. Not because of its accuracy – I was a black teenage girl from London, not a white New Yorker like the flashback version of Monica Geller from *Friends* – but because he was acknowledging my fatness out loud when I'd tried so hard for years to avoid any mention of it.

More than avoided, I had tried to conceal it. I compressed my gut under Spanx and restrictive vests to marginally shrink my unsightly body. When I got home after school, my skin would be bruised from the pressure. I believed that squeezing myself into trousers that didn't fit me, with sharp zips that never did up and pinched at the skin on my belly, would save me from petty comments like Peter's.

"How original," I replied wryly, garnering a few nervous laughs from my friends. He sauntered off unaffected. We both knew that deep down, he'd got to me. I knew I was fat, but he had made me feel ashamed. I began to think that maybe I needed the jibes from distant cousins or unimaginative slights from boys at school. It would make me skinny eventually, wouldn't it?

It didn't, though. The fat didn't fall away. Quite frankly, all those comments and looks did was drive me to extremes. I'd hoover up junk food, cheese, anything, in the early hours of the morning, and quietly attempt to give it all back to the toilet bowl the next day. Shame is usually for the benefit of the people dishing it out, not those on the receiving end.

"Shame is usually for the benefit of the people dishing it out, not those on the receiving end."

Supposedly well-meaning comments began to sting. "Don't wear those trousers, they don't flatter you!" hurt as much as someone yelling, "Drape yourself in dowdy camouflage so I don't have to look at your huge, flabby arse!" The people saying this thought being fat was like being a walking, talking bad habit, and that they, the caring support systems, would cut that "gross behaviour" out with tough love. Except it wasn't love at all.

In some ways, I don't blame people who think it is kind to make others feel bad for the bodies they live and breathe in every day. Like me, they have been taught that fat people, especially women, especially the dark ones, are an embarrassment. We've all been trained to see some people and traits as of less value than others. Weight, body shape, gender, disability, sexuality and the colour of your skin are just some of the things people think they can judge you on.

Look at any of our most popular television shows, movies, magazine covers or music artists. You'll rarely see girls who look like me, with hair as kinky and as short as mine, or with dark, writhing stretch marks on their bellies. But others see people like them celebrated every day. These lucky individuals often have the luxury of being excluded from the violent reactions so many of us have to endure because of who we are. On the rare occasion where they feel in a minority or are vulnerable, they deflect that experience. Some variation of the response "At least I'm not as fat/black/etc. as you" is usually the only way they know how to deal with it.

As much as people sincerely believe that humiliation can be a force for good, it's not a foolproof tactic. I don't like reading through my diaries from this period because for every stupid crush, argument or innocent observation, there are three or four entries about self-loathing. Shame didn't curb my secret binge-eating. It ripped my self-esteem from limb to limb, roll to roll, stretch mark to stretch mark. The smallness of most of my friends and the frequent comments from my own parents and sisters to strangers on the street reminded me of what I was. Every. Single. Day. All I could think about was becoming a skinnier, "better" version of myself. And by attempting to starve myself into a body that would invite less scrutiny, I was damaging both my mental and physical health.

But sometimes if I spent enough time alone, away from the poorly hidden looks of pity or ridicule from people who made it their mission to make me feel uncomfortable, I'd almost forget that I was fat. One day, on a particularly quiet midwinter evening after school, I stopped worrying completely. My mother was at work, giving me free rein of the house. After fixing my usual after-school snack, I decided to use my time to do something different: I danced. Picking up a CD from my rather eclectic selection of favourite artists, I placed it in the CD tray on our powerful hi-fi system, pushed it closed, and blasted out an album I knew I was supposed to have left in 1999: Christina Aguilera's self-titled debut album. By track five, "Come On Over Baby", I was sweating, smiling, screaming the pop lyrics into the ceiling of the living room, and beaming at myself in our large living-room mirror.

By pushing that all-consuming hate aside for an hour or so, it was as if I had given myself permission to look at my body and come out the other side with a new-found love for it. That was when I was able to write a poem that acknowledged how I felt about my body at the same time as looking at it objectively.

"I had given myself permission to look at my body and come out the other side with a new-found love for it."

Bulbous soft,
it droops slightly,
protrudes from my torso.
The underside boasts smooth,
raised marks of stressed skin, not
darkened yet,
but on their way.
Malleable,
it pours into position
with every pull of my limbs
it swims the length of the threads
which encase it,
or the sheets which entice it,
or the air
that it swims through obtrusively
prior to the remaining features on
my body.
It precedes my breasts –
warm and heavy –
my thighs – thick-thick –
my nose, pinpricked
with a small silver stud.
Tummy.
Stomach.
Gut.
Gluttonous blob.

Poem: age 15

My belly that had never been flat, that sagged, that had stretch marks, was now, as I described it, a piece of art to be studied, even admired. I'm in awe of my fifteen-year-old self for finding the strength to be that honest.

With this poem, I'd started the journey of forgiving myself for being me. Eventually, the heat of embarrassment that usually rose within me whenever someone stared at my cellulite for too long, or told me I "actually had such a pretty face", as if they were giving me a compliment, became a need for me to defend myself. When during a flying visit, a neighbour suggested that I become "a model, but just for the face, of course", a quiet voice in my head told her that I could be a model full stop.

So I told her, politely, why her words weren't as kind as she thought. And although the backhanded compliments from people too blinded by conventional beauty standards to see the beauty in people like me continued to come, they hurt less the more I saw myself – really saw myself – for who I was. I was a person worth listening to, worth loving, with as much beauty on the outside as she had on the inside.

"I was a person worth listening to, worth loving,

with as much beauty on the outside as she had on the inside."

Physical and mental health often work together, and if you happen to be able to achieve both, this is wonderful. But using shame to achieve them isn't the way to do it. And sometimes the best way to learn to leave shame behind is seeing others lead by example.

A couple of years later, I discovered one of social media's rarest charms: a supportive niche community made up of a whole host of fat people who had also grown tired of being told they should hate everything about themselves. For the first time, I saw myself in others: bodies of varying shapes and colours proudly on display, no roll concealed, nobody better or worse than another. They were all different, and that was OK. Stunning, in fact. I came across post after post telling me it was fine to look the way I did – that fatness itself wasn't ugly; other people's violent loathing of it was. And within months of reminding myself of that on a daily basis, I believed it too.

If you've ever had to do the work of teaching yourself, second by second, day by day, to love yourself, you'll know that when you do eventually achieve something resembling self-acceptance, it almost feels as if it has come out of nowhere.

That's what it felt like when I put on a bikini for the first time since I was a child. Inspired by the boldness of beautiful, fat black bloggers, I wore it – a white and purple floral high-waisted two-piece from New Look – during a trip to Barbados when I was nineteen. Before that, I'd always worn shorts over my swimming costume: long enough to cover the cellulite on my thighs, big enough to hide my belly from view. But I'd always felt uncomfortable in them.

And because I let myself wear what I wanted and stopped putting other people's possible reactions to the way I looked first, I felt comfortable in public for the first time in ages. I ran happily across the sand with my older sisters, not caring one bit about whether my shaking thighs were offensive to anyone. I even allowed myself the small luxury of pulling the bottoms down slightly, so I could tan my stomach. And it continued that way.

One day I was wearing more layers than my limbs could comfortably move in, all in an effort to hide my fat from the world; the next, I was flaunting it all in tiny crop tops at the height of summer, just because I could.

So when I reluctantly peek at the past, and look beyond the debilitating shyness and shame I so permanently lived with, I wish I'd had someone to share that same knowledge with me much earlier, at primary school, perhaps, before the idea that I was essentially ugly would cloud my every thought for years on end.

So I'll say it now to you, instead.

As you've probably already noticed, people will say things about you. Whether you are tall, short, fat or thin, some people think they have a right to comment on your body. And they might say mean, gross and disgusting things that no one should say to anyone. People can be awful, and although it doesn't justify it, it is usually because they're struggling too. But you should hold on to the spark inside of you that you know is there. Embrace the power that occasionally gives you a gleeful shiver when you look at your body in the mirror. In the privacy of your own room, a haven for discovering new parts of yourself, cling to the feeling of being drawn to yourself in ways that perhaps no one else has. If I were you, I'd shake your tummy, stomach, gut, or whatever you're insecure about, with glorious abandon, and embrace that joyful sensation. Hold on to it. It'll come in handy in a few years, trust me.

"You should hold on to the spark inside of you that you know is there."

THE LESSON
OF DANCE
SCHOOL

THE DREAM
THAT WASN'T
A DREAM

written by

CHARLIE
BRINKHURST-CUFF

When I was growing up, I was convinced I was going to be a dancer. Like so many little girls, I started ballet lessons when I was a toddler, drawn in by the flounce and the pink silk. I then progressed to tap and from there to the bouncy curls and stiff pleats of Irish dancing – briefly becoming an All England champion when I was seven.

I adored the fake crystal tiara I wore when I was competing, but dancing was about more than just the outfits. When I was dancing well, I could rid the shyness from my body. It was exhilarating to win competitions and thrilling to push my body to its limits: how far could I stretch? How high could I leap? How fast could I kick my legs? I was naturally an anxious child, but when I was dancing I felt brave.

Although I pretty much stopped going to lessons when I was about ten and my family moved from London to Scotland (the classes were expensive and far away in Edinburgh), my dream lived on. I would imagine myself, taut and poised and tall, pirouetting around a sprung dance floor in front of a glistening mirror and a barre. I would leap and prance around my bedroom and watch dance movies like *Fame*, *Breakin'*, *Hairspray* (eighties), *Strictly Ballroom* (nineties), *Billy Elliot*, *Honey* and

"When I was dancing well, I could rid the shyness from my body."

Step Up (noughties) on the stuttering wall projector my parents had instead of a TV.

When I started at Edinburgh's Broughton High School at eleven, it was with a flutter of anticipation. At that time it was a crumbling state school with a reputation for bullying and it stood in the shadow of a very exclusive private school that looked like Hogwarts. But the special thing about Broughton was that it focused on the performing arts, just like the school in *Fame*. You could trot down the corridors to the sound of trumpets, timpani, trombones and occasionally the odd bagpipe, or spy the glamorous older girls with their hair slicked back into buns, making their way to dance lessons in the upstairs studio.

I wanted to be like those dancers, but first I had to audition. Pass the audition and it meant glorious after-school dance clubs, cute outfits and the thrill of performances. It even meant getting to skip academic lessons to dance instead. Fail and – in my eyes at least – that dream would be over. My innate ability and passion for dance would shine through, I thought on the day of auditions. It wouldn't matter that I hadn't been to a dance lesson in a while. I was born to be a dancer.

On the day of the audition, I was terrified. Everything felt hot. My shorts were too tight, my tights too slippery and my bumpy locs couldn't be neatened into a smooth bun, especially after my hairband broke.

The audition started and I took a deep breath and tried to banish my worries. We did our stretches, and I scooped down to touch the floor with ease, then slid into smooth splits. It was going OK but still I ignored the big mirror that I'd once been so desperate to dance in front of.

Then the teacher asked to see our ballet skills: first position, second position, third. Elsewhere in the studio, I could see my friends in their ballet shoes, holding on to the barre like they were born to be there. But I had done ballet for only a couple of years as a very young child and I couldn't remember where to set my feet. Trying not to panic, in the break between the positions, I decided to show off my flexibility and trialled some Irish dancing moves that I hoped might impress the teachers.

But when it came to the hip hop element of the audition and we were tasked with learning some steps to a fast beat, I found myself sliding around the floor like a baby elephant. I was flustered and painfully aware that I was out of my depth. I should've stopped to take off my tights and dance barefoot, but thanks to the brand new hairs sprouting on my legs, I was too ashamed. I soldiered slippily on, praying that I wouldn't be the worst in the room.

"I found myself sliding around the floor like a baby elephant."

The dream wasn't to be. When I received the letter saying that I didn't get into dance school I cried for days.

All of my friends who auditioned got in. I was the only one out of my group who didn't. And the pain of that failure, like a break-up, lasted long afterwards. "When I used to go and see my friends' dance shows," wrote my fourteen-year-old self in my diary, three years on from the audition, "I used to sit there and cry in the audience, wishing I could be up there with them."

Really, by then, I no longer wanted to dance. I had failed at something I thought I might have a talent for. I could have gone to dance lessons outside of school, but besides being very expensive, the little confidence I had was gone. How could I be a dancer if I couldn't learn steps quickly and even the thought of dancing in front of an audience made my heart beat like a marching band drum? I wrote in my diary:

Just now, I put on some music and danced for about half an hour, just to myself. But then I got depressed, because I know I'll never be a dancer, that I'm the wrong shape and figure, that it's too late for me to learn how to dance professionally, that I'm too shy to dance in front of anyone, to let myself go, that I don't pick up dance

moves quick enough, that although I'm
flexible, I'm just not good enough – I
shall never be a dancer, instead I'll go to
university; do English or History; become
a journalist, but all the while, lurking in
the back of my mind will be this feeling of
wanting to move and dance...

Diary entry: age 14

Failing the audition meant that dance suddenly
became associated with lots of negative emotions which
ended up feeding into my insecurities about my race, my
body and the way I looked. In another diary entry,
I bemoan a friend who says that she wants to weigh
"eight and a half stone" because, in part, "she's black!
Our bodies don't go that skinny!" The diversity of body
shapes among the black community was not something I
knew about in ninety-eight per cent white Scotland where,
my diary also notes, "I've been called paki, nigger,
mongrel, 'black bin bag', and had a thousand digs made
at me before because of the colour of my skin".

Just as I felt too embarrassed to take off my tights
during that audition, the following years would see me
become more and more concerned about my body
and its visible blackness; it would ultimately be what I
blamed for the failure of my dream. It wasn't until much

later that I discovered there were black ballet dancers with athletic figures like Misty Copeland and girls who danced a fusion of ballet and hip hop known as hiplet.

I didn't achieve my dream of becoming a dancer, but I'm sure that when I wrote that entry, I thought going to university was just as much of an improbable dream. No one in my immediate family had ever been to university and I didn't think I was smart or capable enough to become a journalist. Three years on from this entry I wasn't dancing, but I was very happily expanding my mind while studying English literature at university.

Ten years on from this entry, I am a journalist who writes for a living – and while it's been a rollercoaster journey, I have travelled all over the world, interviewed my heroes, learned so many things and helped people in all kinds of ways. You could say that when I wrote that diary entry I actually knew myself pretty well; we shouldn't underestimate our teenage selves. By the time you're a teenager, you've formed most of the parts of yourself that will stay with you for life. I predicted my future; I achieved another of my dreams.

But the one thing I got wrong in that diary entry? I don't think about dancing much at all these days. As I left my teens I discovered, through reading and watching interviews with

"I predicted my future; I achieved another of my dreams."

dancers, that dancing wouldn't have always been the fun or glamorous life I had imagined. The dream I had held close for so many years no longer seemed like a dream I actually wanted to live. And that is a big part of growing up: learning to let go of some of the things we thought defined us, especially if they are making us unhappy.

One of the beautiful things that has happened as I've grown older is a love for my body. I remember the first sticky-floored club nights out I had in Edinburgh, tottering around in high heels, unsteady on rough seas of possibility as to who we might "get with" that evening before our midnight curfews kicked in or the bouncers realized we'd all used the same ID. Back then, the thought of dancing in a club, even to music I thought I liked, was pretty terrifying. I shuffled and shimmied like the awkward wallflower I was railing against inside,

"The dream I had held close for so many years no longer seemed like a dream I actually wanted to live.

only freed by a few shots of tequila, and even then not really knowing how to move my body to this type of high-paced electronic dance music.

It wasn't until the year I moved away from Scotland to London for university that I began to find a black community I could resonate with and a type of music I could feel. Seventeen, at a weird party in London, someone put on dancehall, Beenie Man's "I'm Drinking/Rum & Red Bull", and my friends and I were suddenly dancing with men old enough to know better and having the time of our lives. For the first time in years, I felt like I could dance again. I could whine and move the bum I had once despised. No longer was I going to hide it in flared skirts or with jumpers tied around my waist. My dream of dancing was gone, but I decided I would become a cheerleader at university and put my naturally athletic body shape to use.

And that is a big part of growing up."

One of the reasons why I kept a diary for so many years was so I didn't forget what it felt like to be a young person. I never wanted to feel derision for the emotions my younger self went through. My diary held my hand into my future: a literal book of words that shaped me and that I had shaped in turn. And when I read back through those entries, while I can recognize a hint of drama, there is no mockery or self-pity. My failure to become a dancer was something I felt deeply. After a pretty blissful childhood, it was a privileged wake-up call that the world wouldn't always be as kind as I had once thought. But looking back and picturing my younger self, I am so glad to be where I am today, doing something that in many ways is more scary and bold than any of my other dreams could have been. My reasons for quitting dancing were wrong because they were tied up in my insecurities, but so were my reasons for wanting to be a dancer: I wanted to fit in. With journalism, I've been forced to stand out. I've had plenty more knocks on this career path, but I've brought myself back from them, because this is my dream now.

Our dreams and aspirations aren't always what they seem. They are veiled in our insecurities and our egos; they are not big or brave enough to ever fulfil us. Dancing can be beautiful, fun and joyful, but it is only a footnote in my story and one of many dreams.

"I've had plenty more knocks on this career path, but I've brought myself back from them, because this is my dream now."

THE UNCOOL GIRL'S MANIFESTO

HOW TO HANG ON IN THERE

written by

GRACE HOLLIDAY

Hey, uncool girl. Wanna come to a party with me?

It's New Year's Eve, 2004. See the skinny mixed-race brunette in the corner? That's fourteen-year-old me. I've got hairy eyebrows, bony wrists and the only thing inside my bra right now is scrunched-up tissues. There couldn't be a bigger gap between me and the cool girls at school.

Mum's friend is asking me questions. Her breasts are perhaps a little too perky to be real, but who knows – they look far better than mine. She asks me about school, so I give her the only answer I can think of: "It's fine, thanks."

"Enjoy it," she replies, wine sloshing in her glass as she leans forward. "These are the best years of your life."

Then off she goes, tissue-less bra first. In response to my white lie, she has told a whopper. Teenage years are *not* the best years of your life. They can be the absolute pits.

But all you have to do, uncool girl, is hang on in there. If I did it, so can you.

Just like me, you're the uncool girl who feels like she doesn't quite fit in anywhere, yet seems to stand out for all the wrong reasons. Maybe you have an unusual hobby, or a strict curfew, or only go camping in Cleethorpes for your summer holidays. But despite

"I have no idea who came up with the rule

this, you've got big ambitions and even bigger dreams. You're looking towards the future. I wish fourteen-year-old me could link arms with you and give you a nudge and a smile. I think we'd get on.

Let's leave this party and head upstairs, uncool girl, and sit on my bed for a bit. I spent most of my teenage years in my bedroom, aside from school. Now, make yourself comfy: we're going to have a chat about the next few years. You probably feel that this should be a period filled with fun, friends and wild parties. You are meant to snog boys and pass your exams with flying colours (though probably not at the same time!).

I have no idea who came up with the rule that your teenage years are the best years of your life. Some misty-eyed man, probably, remembering endless rugby games at boarding school. No one who lives in reality, that's for sure – and certainly putting pressure on yourself to enjoy these years really doesn't help.

For us uncool girls, our expectations of what life should be and the reality don't quite match up. Let's take a look at my teenage years and I'll show you how they were different from all those make-believe expectations. But don't worry: it doesn't mean that the years after won't be amazing. It is all about hanging on in there.

that your teenage years are the best years of your life."

I grew up in Doncaster, South Yorkshire. I've never really felt like I fitted in. My family was one of two non-white families in our village. I had two much older siblings – by eight and ten years – but they had both left for university by the time I was ten.

I didn't really have a social life, and certainly no boyfriend. Any boys I knew fancied Amanda, my best friend, with her long, thick blonde hair and curvy hips. After school, everyone hung out outside the corner shop, sharing fags, bottles of Lambrini and saliva. Even if I had been invited, I wouldn't have been allowed out. My strict dad had set me a bedtime of 8 p.m. (which he generously extended to 9 p.m. when I turned sixteen – thanks, Dad). At this point in my life, my best chance of partying was at my seven-year-old cousin's bowling party.

My days were spent at school and my nights here, on this bed, reading and writing. But I had a plan. I was going to get out, just like my siblings had done. Out of this bedroom. Out of my school. Out of my small village. Out was a place where reading books was cool, not nerdy. Where other people loved

> **"At this point in my life, my best chance of partying was at my seven-year-old cousin's bowling party."**

Noughts & Crosses by Malorie Blackman. Out was university, where I could drop maths and science and study a subject that I loved and was good at. Out was where I would find real friends and people who looked like me with big noses and hairy arms. Out was going to be so good.

> **Expectation: You need perfect grades and a dream career**
> **Reality: You have no idea what your dream career is**

Doing well at school was a huge part of my plan to get out, but there were subjects I struggled with. In maths, Mr Woodward would stand over me as the numbers swayed in front of my eyes, jumbling up against my will. I adored art but could barely draw a straight line. I loved dance, but even a basic step-step-leap had me tripping over my own feet. The only place I ever felt comfortable was in English, reading books and writing about them.

So far so good: it meant I could become a writer. But I couldn't be more specific than that. Journalist? English teacher? Novelist? I wasn't alone; most of my friends had no idea what to do next or how to get there (and some of them still aren't sure now). Pressure from teachers and family to decide really didn't help either.

*Expectation: You will have a life of independence
and freedom*
*Reality: You spend most of your time making lists
in your bedroom*

TV shows like Sex Education and Pretty Little Liars
make the teenage years look so free and fun. Yet that
kind of independence always felt like something other
people had: my parents, my siblings, the cool kids.
They had freedom and I had ... well, I had lists.

Here's one I wrote in my diary in September 2005,
when I was fifteen.

New Academic Year Resolutions
- **Shower every other day.**
- **Do housework often and willingly.**
- **Eat 5 fruit/veg per day.**
- **Drink 7/8 glasses of water.**
- **Eat minimal junk food.**
- **Do HWK straight after school.**
- **Keep room clean and tidy.**
- **Swim fortnightly and gym weekly.**
- **Treats of good TV and fave chocolate.**

Diary entry: age 15

Don't laugh! I loved my lists. I wrote them for
everything: to-do lists, motivational lists, resolution lists,
new year lists. I'd kept a diary ever since I could write,
and lists seemed like the next logical, adult step.

When I look back now, uncool girl, I can see something very clearly. These expectations, real or imaginary, and lists of what I should be doing heaped huge pressure on my teenage shoulders. I was trying to achieve things that even now, when I'm nearly thirty, I would struggle with.

So I want to tell you, uncool girl, not to do the same. Don't get swept away by thinking that you have to live the lives you see on Instagram to be happy. Do what makes you joyful. Don't worry if you are different from everyone else. You'll find people like you soon.

As it turned out, I didn't need to get straight As in every single subject to land a great job. And when Mr Woodward said, "You'll need maths when you're an adult – you don't walk about with a calculator in your pocket!" he simply didn't know that iPhones were coming.

All that time spent in my bedroom helped me to find something I truly love. Books were my escape, the characters were my friends and their adventures fired my imagination. I now write and teach for a living. I've just been travelling around Sri Lanka, where I had to write a magazine article about staying at a gorgeous resort,

"Don't get swept away by thinking that you have to live the lives you see on Instagram to be happy."

eating delicious food and having daily massages. What I do now is more exciting and fulfilling than my wildest of bedroom daydreams.

With this in mind, I can't even be cross with Dad any more. I know he wanted the best for me and he felt an 8 p.m. bedtime was the way to make that happen. So *not* sarcastically this time: thanks, Dad.

And my love life? At sixteen, I started a new school and I auditioned for the school play *Blood Brothers*. I was cast as Mrs Lyons. The guy who played Mr Lyons? He was gorgeous, generous, kind and funny. Did I mention gorgeous? He couldn't care less about my eyebrows, and as for my boobs, well, he was more of a bum guy anyway. Now he's my husband and we share a house in Leeds, a city I adore. That New Year's Eve, I never would have dreamed that the right guy was out there. But actually I just hadn't met him yet.

Writing lists, however, has become a lifelong habit. But I'm far kinder to myself today than when I was a teenager. If I had to rewrite that list I wrote when I was fifteen, it would read very differently:

- **Wash my hair every other day. Dry shampoo habit = expensive.**
- **Do housework whenever I can be bothered (aka never).**
- **Eat more fruit and veg. Strawberry jam in doughnuts does not count.**

- *Drink 4 glasses of water a day.*
- *Eat more home-cooked meals and less microwaveable meals, even when they're really nice ones in the reduced aisle of Marks & Spencer.*
- *Gym weekly. Swim three times a year.*
- *Treats of good TV, fave chocolate, lie-ins on Sundays.*

I will never do housework often and willingly, but that makes me human, not lazy. Self-awareness, though often mortifying, is an important skill to have. My lists help me figure out what makes me happy. There is huge value, uncool girl, in figuring out what gives you joy. You might not have freedom today, but that doesn't mean you can't plan for once it arrives. When that time comes, you'll appreciate it even more. Trust me.

"You might not have freedom today, but that doesn't mean you can't plan for once it arrives."

To get you through these years, I want to share with you "The Uncool Girl's Manifesto". It's our declaration, just between you and me, of all the good things we promise to believe are out there for us.

THE UNCOOL GIRL'S
MANIFESTO

I WILL REMEMBER THAT HAPPY TIMES AND FREEDOM ARE AHEAD

Enjoy what you can today, and make plans for your tomorrow. The world is wide and it needs your ideas, your perspective and your personality. It needs you.

I WILL TRUST THAT MY PEOPLE ARE OUT THERE

Maybe your friends are waiting at university or college. Maybe they'll turn up at the next school play auditions and one of them might propose to you one day. I don't know. But I do know this: your people can't wait to meet you either.

I WILL TREAT MYSELF KINDLY

There is enough pressure on your shoulders from adults, teachers, school, hormones and social media without adding even more on yourself. Be kind to yourself. Treat yourself like you would your best friend.

I WILL BELIEVE THAT COOL IS JUST A WORD, AND NOTHING MORE

Cool and uncool are definitions that will soon become utterly meaningless. You get to decide your own label, and it's now time to shake off "uncool". You are so, so much more than that. Kind? Hilarious? Smart? Creative? That's the wonderful thing about life – you get to decide who you are.

It's going to get better, sweet girl. You're doing great. Just hang on in there.

about
gal-dem

about gal-dem

gal-dem is a platform created and produced by women and non-binary people of colour for everyone to enjoy.

gal-dem addresses inequality and misrepresentation through platforming the creative and editorial work of young women and non-binary people of colour across fashion, lifestyle, politics, music, arts and opinion. As well as their digital platform, they publish an annual print magazine. They've interviewed many influential women and non-binary people of colour, including Oprah, Mel B, Angie Thomas and Roxane Gay.

gal-dem has worked on collaborations with a huge range of partners, including the Victoria and Albert Museum, the Tate Modern, Converse and Glossier. In August 2018 gal-dem took over the *Guardian Weekend* magazine.

Find them online: www.gal-dem.com
Follow them on Instagram and Twitter:
@galdemzine

yumna al-arashi

Yumna Al-Arashi is a Yemeni-Egyptian-American photographer, film-maker and writer based in London. She was raised in Washington DC and studied social inquiry at The New School in NYC. Her work has appeared on billboards and in magazines, books, museums and galleries around the world. When she's not pursuing her childhood dreams of becoming an artist, she's probably walking through a forest, or swimming in the ocean.

@yumna

samanthi theminimulle

Samanthi Theminimulle was born and raised in south London. She has been an editor at gal-dem. Now Samanthi mostly writes for herself, reflecting on her experiences of being a British Sri Lankan woman. She is an avid drinker of ginger tea and loves purchasing discounted trainers.

nina dahmani

Nina Dahmani (not her real name) was born in Jakarta, raised in Surrey and now lives in London. She studied art history at UCL and currently works in advertising. She has been producing content for gal-dem for a number of years. As well as absorbing and arranging words, Nina finds great joy in eating, cooking, sharing, discovering and discussing food – the spicier the better!

niellah arboine

Niellah Arboine was born and raised in south London. She studied English literature and creative writing at Aberystwyth University and her work can be found in *The Independent*, *Bustle*, *i-D* and *Time Out*. In 2018 she wrote her first play for Theatre Uncut. Niellah is a former music scholar and played the French horn at school because it was a left-handed instrument.

@niellaharboine

sara jafari

Sara Jafari was born in Hull and now lives in south London. She works in publishing and in her spare time runs her own literary and arts magazine, *TOKEN Magazine*. She wrote her first book about wizards, forbidden love and Muslim parents when she was fifteen years old. She is a London Writers Awards winner and has had her work published in numerous publications.

@sarajafari

kuchenga

KUCHENGA is a north London native who now lives in Brighton (aka North London-on-Sea). She is a journalist and writer whose work has featured in *i-D*, *Harper's Bazaar* and *Vogue* and the acclaimed anthology *To My Trans Sisters*. She named her dog Nene after a Real Housewife of Atlanta, but actually wants to be the first black Real Housewife of Beverly Hills.

@kuchengcheng

layale

Layale (not her real name) was born and raised in the North of England in a conservative Muslim family. She juggles writing for national publications about race, religion and sexual violence with her day job in communications. She appears under a pseudonym because, despite the many taboos she has dismantled with her parents, writing publicly about sex and relationships would be one step too far – and she's not going to risk losing her mum's curry (and love) for ever.

leah cowan

Leah Cowan was born in the West Midlands and now lives in London. She is the politics editor at gal-dem and has written for *Vice UK*, *The Occupied Times*, *Media Diversified* and the *Guardian*. She works in the ending violence against women and girls (VAWG) sector, and supports the abolition of immigration detention, deportation and the prison industrial complex. Growing up she enjoyed reading books about witches and magic and still does today.

@la_cowan

candace lee camacho

Candace Lee Camacho, professionally known as duendita, is an artist from Queens, New York. Currently based between NYC and Berlin, she spends her time songwriting, singing and birdwatching. Her debut EP *direct line to My Creator* (2018) was independently released to critical acclaim.

@duendita95

liv little

Liv Little is a curator, audio producer and the founder of gal-dem. She has worked as a digital executive in commissioning at the BBC and as a contributing editor for *ELLE UK*. Liv is obsessed with telling people's stories across all mediums including audio, video, art and discussion. Her mum gave her the nickname Little Fish because she has loved swimming since she was young.

@livlittle

kemi alemoru

Kemi Alemoru grew up writing stories for her friends and teachers in Manchester. Currently based in south London, she studied magazine journalism at City University, before working in youth culture journalism and then joining gal-dem as features editor. She also freelances for publications such as *Riposte* and *AnOther Man*, airing news and her views. She is an essayist in *Mother Country*, where she writes about her Windrush lineage.

@kemioliviax

kuba shand-baptiste

Kuba Shand-Baptiste was born, raised and still resides in Kensal Rise, north-west London. She is gal-dem's chief sub-editor, and a commissioning editor and columnist at the *Independent*. She has an MA in newspaper journalism, and is working on a book project about her local area's ties to the Jamaican community. As a teenager, Kuba played a tenor horn, but most people mistook it for a tuba – you can imagine how much fun her peers had with that one.

@kubared

charlie brinkhurst-cuff

Charlie Brinkhurst-Cuff is an award-winning writer, editor and columnist of Jamaican-Cuban heritage, and writes about issues surrounding race, social justice and media. She oversees the editorial output of gal-dem. In 2018 she edited *Mother Country*, a book about the Windrush generation and their descendants. She grew up in Edinburgh but (annoyingly) doesn't have a Scottish accent. Her childhood dream was to become a professional dancer, but she's glad she's a journalist instead.

@charliebcuff

grace holliday

Grace Holliday was raised in South Yorkshire, but after a decade trying out various cities she finally settled in Leeds, where she is a freelance journalist and journalism lecturer. She has written for the *Guardian*, *Grazia* and *BuzzFeed*. Grace believes meeting the love of your life as a teenager is totally possible (she did!) and breaking up with them to go to uni and *find yourself* is also cool.

@graceholliday
@gracehollidayfreelancer

jess nash

Jess Nash was born in south London and now lives a stone's throw from where she grew up. An avid daydreamer and momentary basketballer, she has turned her lifelong love of drawing, culture and staring into space into her illustration practice. Jess has had the pleasure of drawing for Penguin Random House UK, gal-dem and *The Good Journal*.

@jess__nash

help and
information

In these essays, we've written honestly about some of the difficult and challenging things that we've experienced growing up. If there are issues in this book that affect you, or someone you know, these organizations will be able to offer information and support.

General help and support

ChildLine
www.childline.org.uk

Samaritans
www.samaritans.org

Imkaan
www.imkaan.org.uk

Mental Health

Mind
www.mind.org.uk

The Black, African and Asian Therapy Network
www.baatn.org.uk

Sikh Your Mind
www.sikhyourmind.com

White Swan Foundation
www.whiteswanfoundation.org

Drugs

Frank
www.talktofrank.com

Bullying

Bullying UK
www.bullying.co.uk

Kidscape
www.kidscape.org.uk

Sex and relationships

Naz
www.naz.org.uk

Rape Crisis England and Wales
www.rapecrisis.org.uk

LGBT+ support

Young Stonewall
www.youngstonewall.org.uk

Galop
www.galop.org.uk

Mermaids UK
www.mermaidsuk.org.uk

Eating Disorders

Beat
www.beateatingdisorders.org.uk

If you live outside of the UK, there will be other international organizations that can help you. Do be aware that content on these websites may change.